teach yourself... PASCAL

MARK GOODWIN

ADVANCED COMPUTER BOOKS

MIS: PRESS

D1597460

© 1990 by Management Information Source, Inc.

P.O Box 5277
Portland, Oregon 97208-5277

First Printing
ISBN 1-55828-055-3
Library of Congress Catalog Card Number 90-13375

Printed in the United States of America

TRADEMARKS

IBM is a trademark of International Business Machines Corporation.
Microsoft, MS, MS-DOS, and QuickPascal are trademarks of Microsoft Corporation.
Turbo Pascal is a trademark of Borland International, Inc.

To Baby: the newest member of my wonderful family.

Contents

Figures xiii

Introduction xix

CHAPTER 1. A SIMPLE FIRST PROGRAM.. 1

Lesson 1. The Basic Components of the
 Pascal Programming Language 1

Lesson 2. A First Program 7

CHAPTER 2. PREDEFINED DATA TYPES 11

Lesson 3. Integers 11

Lesson 4. Real Numbers 16

Lesson 5. Booleans 19

Lesson 6. Characters 21

Lesson 7. Strings 24

CHAPTER 3. THE PASCAL OPERATORS.. 29

Lesson 8. The Assignment Operator 29

Lesson 9. The Unary Plus Operator 31

Lesson 10. The Unary Minus Operator 32

Contents

Lesson 11. The Addition Operator 33

Lesson 12. The Subtraction Operator 34

Lesson 13. The Multiplication Operator 35

Lesson 14. The Real Number Division Operator 36

Lesson 15. The Integer Division Operator 38

Lesson 16. The Remainder Operator 39

Lesson 17. The Logical Negation Operator 40

Lesson 18. The Logical And Operator 41

Lesson 19. The Logical Or Operator 43

Lesson 20. The Exclusive Or Operator 44

Lesson 21. The Bitwise Negation Operator 46

Lesson 22. The Bitwise And Operator 48

Lesson 23. The Bitwise Or Operator 49

Lesson 24. The Bitwise Exclusive Or Operator 51

Lesson 25. The Bitwise Shift Left Operator 52

Lesson 26. The Bitwise Shift Right Operator 53

Lesson 27. The String Concatenation Operator 55

Lesson 28. The Equal To Operator 56

Lesson 29. The Not Equal To Operator 57

Lesson 30. The Greater Than Operator 58

Lesson 31. The Greater Than Or Equal To Operator 59

Lesson 32. The Less Than Operator 60

Lesson 33. The Less Than Or Equal To Operator 61

Lesson 34. Operator Precedence 62

CHAPTER 4. PROGRAM FLOW 65

Lesson 35. While Loops 65

Lesson 36. Repeat Loops 67

Lesson 37. For Loops 69

Lesson 38. If Statements 72

Lesson 39. Case Statements 75

Lesson 40. Goto Statements 77

CHAPTER 5. PROCEDURES AND FUNCTIONS 79

Lesson 41. Declaring Procedures and Functions 80

Lesson 42. Function Return Values 83

Lesson 43. Forward Declarations 85

Lesson 44. Local Variables 88

Lesson 45. Scope 91

Lesson 46. Arguments 93

Lesson 47. Nested Procedures and Functions 95

Lesson 48. Recursion 97

CHAPTER 6. USER-DEFINED DATA TYPES 101

Lesson 49. Enumerated Data Types 101

Contents

Lesson 50. The Dec Procedure 103

Lesson 51. The Inc Procedure 104

Lesson 52. The Pred Function 106

Lesson 53. The Succ Function 107

Lesson 54. Subranges 108

Lesson 55. Sets 110

Lesson 56. The Set Equal To Operator 111

Lesson 57. The Set Not Equal To Operator 112

Lesson 58. The Set Less Than Or Equal To Operator 113

Lesson 59. The Set Greater Than Or Equal To Operator 114

Lesson 60. The Set In Operator 115

Lesson 61. The Set Union Operator 116

Lesson 62. The Set Difference Operator 117

Lesson 63. The Set Intersection Operator 118

CHAPTER 7. ARRAYS 121

Lesson 64. A Simple Array 121

Lesson 65. Typed Constant Arrays 125

Lesson 66. Multi-Dimensional Arrays 126

Lesson 67. Passing Arrays To Procedures and Functions 131

CHAPTER 8. RECORDS 133

Lesson 68. Record Basics 134

Lesson 69. The With Statement 137

Lesson 70. Typed Constant Records 139

Lesson 71. Record Arrays 140

Lesson 72. Field Arrays 142

CHAPTER 9. VARIANT RECORDS 145

Lesson 73. Variant Record Basics 145

CHAPTER 10. POINTERS 151

Lesson 74. Simple Pointers 151

Lesson 75. Array and Record Pointers 154

Lesson 76. Procedure and Function Pointers 157

CHAPTER 11. DYNAMIC MEMORY MANAGEMENT 165

Lesson 77. Allocating and Deallocating Single Data Objects 166

Lesson 78. Allocating and Deallocating Blocks of Memory 167

CHAPTER 12. UNITS 171

Lesson 79. The Uses Statement 172

Lesson 80. Creating a Pascal Unit 173

Lesson 81. Identifiers With the Same Name 176

CHAPTER 13. WORKING WITH STRINGS 179

Lesson 82. The String Concatenation Function 179

Lesson 83. The Pascal Copy Function 180

Lesson 84. The Pascal Delete Procedure 181

Contents

Lesson 85. The Pascal Insert Procedure 182

Lesson 86. The Pascal Pos Function 183

CHAPTER 14. CONSOLE INPUT/OUTPUT 185

Lesson 87. The Write and Writeln Procedures 185

Lesson 88. The Read and Readln Procedures 187

Lesson 89. Formatted Output 188

CHAPTER 15. TEXT FILE INPUT/OUTPUT 191

Lesson 90. Text Files 192

Lesson 91. Error Trapping 196

CHAPTER 16. BINARY FILE INPUT/OUTPUT 199

Lesson 92. Typed Binary Files 200

Lesson 93. Untyped Binary Files 203

**CHAPTER 17. OBJECT-ORIENTED PROGRAMMING IN
QUICKPASCAL** 209

Lesson 94. Encapsulation 209

Lesson 95. Inheritance 216

Lesson 96. Polymorphism 220

**CHAPTER 18. OBJECT-ORIENTED PROGRAMMING IN
TURBO PASCAL** 225

Lesson 97. Encapsulation 225

Lesson 98. Inheritance 231

Lesson 99. Polymorphism 235

Lesson 100. Dynamic Objects 240

Index 247

Figures

Chapter 1

1-1.	The Turbo Pascal keywords	2
1-2.	The QuickPascal keywords	2
1-3.	The Pascal operators	5

Chapter 2

2-1.	The hexadecimal number system (base 16)	12
2-2.	The Pascal integer types	13
2-3.	Defining an integer variable	13
2-4.	Defining a typed integer constant	14
2-5.	The Pascal real number types	16
2-6.	Defining a real number variable	17
2-7.	Defining a typed real number constant	17
2-8.	Defining a boolean variable	19
2-9.	Defining a typed boolean constant	20
2-10.	Pascal character data representations	22
2-11.	Defining a character variable	23
2-12.	Defining a typed character constant	23
2-13.	Defining a string variable	25
2-14.	Defining a typed string constant	26

Chapter 3

3-1.	The Pascal assignment operator	30
3-2.	The Pascal unary plus operator	31
3-3.	The Pascal unary minus operator	32

3-4. The Pascal addition operator 33

3-5. The Pascal subtraction operator 34

3-6. The Pascal multiplication operator 35

3-7. The Pascal real number operator 37

3-8. The Pascal integer division operator 38

3-9. The Pascal remainder operator 39

3-10. A logical negation truth table 40

3-11. The Pascal logical negation operator 40

3-12. A logical and truth table 41

3-13. The Pascal logical and operator 42

3-14. A logical or truth table 43

3-15. The Pascal logical or operator 43

3-16. An exclusive or truth table 44

3-17. The Pascal exclusive or operator 45

3-18. A byte of bits 46

3-19. A bitwise negation truth table 46

3-20. The Pascal bitwise negation operator 47

3-21. A bitwise and truth table 48

3-22. The Pascal bitwise and operator 48

3-23. A bitwise or truth table 49

3-24. The Pascal bitwise or operator 50

3-25. A bitwise exclusive or truth table 51

3-26. The Pascal bitwise exclusive or operator 51

3-27. The Pascal shift left operator 52

3-28. The Pascal shift right operator 54

3-29. The Pascal string concatenation operator 55

3-30. The Pascal equal to operator 56

3-31. The Pascal not equal to operator 57

3-32. The Pascal greater than operator 58

3-33. The Pascal greater than or equal to operator 59

3-34. The Pascal less than operator 60

3-35. The Pascal less than or equal to operator 61

3-36. The Pascal operator precedence levels 63

Chapter 4

4-1.   The while keyword 66
4-2.   The repeat keyword 68
4-3.   The for keyword 70
4-4.   The Pascal if..then statement 72
4-5.   The Pascal if..then..else statement 74
4-6.   The Pascal case statement 75
4-7.   The Pascal goto statement 77

Chapter 5

5-1.   A Pascal procedure declaration 81
5-2.   A Pascal function definition 81
5-3.   A forward declaration 87
5-4.   Procedure and function variables 88
5-5.   Nested Pascal procedures and functions 95

Chapter 6

6-1.   Defining a Pascal enumerated data type 102
6-2.   The Pascal dec procedure 103
6-3.   The Pascal inc procedure 105
6-4.   The Pascal pred function 106
6-5.   The Pascal succ function 107
6-6.   Defining a subrange data type 108
6-7.   Defining a Pascal set 110
6-8.   Set assignments 111
6-9.   The Pascal set equal to operator 111
6-10.   The Pascal set not equal to operator 112
6-11.   The Pascal set less than or equal to operator 113
6-12.   The Pascal set greater than or equal to operator 114
6-13.   The Pascal in operator 115
6-14.   The Pascal set union operator 116
6-15.   The Pascal set difference operator 117
6-16.   The Pascal set intersection operator 118

Chapter 7

7-1.   Declaring a Pascal array 123

7-2.   Accessing a Pascal array element 124
7-3.   Declaring a typed constant array 125
7-4.   Declaring a multi-dimensional array 128
7-5.   Declaring a multi-dimensional typed constant 128
7-6.   Accessing a multi-dimensional array element 129
7-7.   Defining an array data type 131

Chapter 8

8-1.   Declaring a Pascal record type 134
8-2.   Declaring a Pascal record field 135
8-3.   Record variable field references 135
8-4.   The Pascal with statement 137
8-5.   Declaring a typed constant record 139
8-6.   Declaring an array of records 141
8-7.   Record array field references 141
8-8.   Declaring a field array 142
8-9.   Field array references 143

Chapter 9

9-1.   Declaring a variant record 148

Chapter 10

10-1.   Declaring a Pascal pointer 152
10-2.   Assigning a variable's address to a pointer 152
10-3.   Assigning the value of one pointer to another 153
10-4.   Assigning nil to a pointer 153
10-5.   Array pointer referencing 154
10-6.   Record pointer referencing 155
10-7.   Defining a procedure data type 157
10-8.   Defining a function data type 158
10-9.   Procedure and function variable assignments 158
10-10. Declaring a pointer pointer 160
10-11. Assigning a procedure or function address to a pointer 161

Chapter 11

11-1.   Allocating memory with the new procedure 166

11-2.   Deallocating memory with the dispose procedure 166
11-3.   Allocating a memory block with getmem 167
11-4.   The Pascal sizeof function 168
11-5.   Deallocating memory with the freemem procedure 168

Chapter 12

12-1.   The Pascal uses statement 172
12-2.   The structure of a Pascal unit 173
12-3.   Conflicting identifier references 176

Chapter 13

13-1.   The Pascal concat function 180
13-2.   The Pascal copy function 181
13-3.   The Pascal delete function 182
13-4.   The Pascal insert procedure 183
13-5.   The Pascal pos function 184

Chapter 14

14-1.   Using the write and writeln procedures for console output 186
14-2.   Using the read and readln procedures for console input 187
14-3.   Formatted write and writeln data items 189

Chapter 15

15-1.   Declaring a text variable 192
15-2.   The Pascal assign procedure 192
15-3.   Opening a file with the rewrite procedure 193
15-4.   Opening a file with the reset procedure 193
15-5.   Opening a file with the append procedure 193
15-6.   Reading file data with the read procedure 194
15-7.   Reading file data with the readln procedure 194
15-8.   Writing file data with the write procedure 194
15-9.   Writing file data with the writeln procedure 195
15-10. Closing a file with the close procedure 195

Chapter 16

16-1.   Declaring a typed binary file variable 200

16-2.   Reading typed binary file data with the read procedure 201
16-3.   Writing typed binary file data with the write procedure 201
16-4.   The Pascal seek procedure 202
16-5.   The Pascal filepos function 202
16-6.   Declaring an untyped binary file variable 204
16-7.   Opening an untyped binary file with the rewrite procedure........... 204
16-8.   Opening an untyped binary file with the reset procedure 205
16-9.   Reading data with the Pascal blockread procedure 205
16-10. Writing data with the Pascal blockwrite procedure 206

Chapter 17

17-1.   Defining a QuickPascal object class 210
17-2.   Defining an object class procedure 211
17-3.   Defining an object class function 212
17-4.   Returning values from an object class function 212
17-5.   Declaring a QuickPascal object 213
17-6.   Referencing instance variables 213
17-7.   Calling an object's method 214
17-8.   Defining a QuickPascal object subclass 217
17-9.   Defining a QuickPascal polymorphic subclass 221
17-10. Calling an inherited method 221

Chapter 18

18-1.   Defining a Turbo Pascal object class 226
18-2.   Defining an object class procedure 227
18-3.   Defining an object class function 227
18-4.   Returning values from an object class function 228
18-5.   Declaring a Turbo Pascal object 228
18-6.   Referencing instance variables 229
18-7.   Calling an object's method 229
18-8.   Defining a Turbo Pascal object subclass 232
18-9.   Defining a Turbo Pascal polymorphic subclass 236
18-10. Calling an inherited virtual method 237
18-11. Dynamically allocating an object with Turbo Pascal 241
18-12. Dynamically deallocating an object with Turbo Pascal 241

Introduction

In the early 1970s, Niklaus Wirth designed a new programming language called Pascal. Mr. Wirth's original intention for the Pascal programming language was to use it as an aid for teaching computer programming. Consequently, it is an excellent programming language for the beginning programmer. Even though Pascal is such a good language for beginners, it also provides more than enough capabilities for even the most advanced programmers.

Today there are two basic types of Pascal: ANSI Pascal and Turbo Pascal. Although ANSI Pascal is supposed to be a standard for all Pascal compilers, Borland's Turbo Pascal is by far the most dominant Pascal compiler in use. Therefore, Turbo Pascal's form of the Pascal programming language is more of a standard than ANSI's. Accordingly, this book is written to teach you how to program in the Turbo Pascal dialect. Microsoft's QuickPascal compiler is also covered in this book, as it adheres to the Turbo Pascal dialect except for in the area of object-oriented programming. Chapter 17 is dedicated to object-oriented programming in QuickPascal, while Chapter 18 covers object-oriented programming in Turbo Pascal.

WHAT THIS BOOK WILL TEACH YOU

This book is intended to teach even a beginning programmer how to program in the Pascal programming language. It covers all of the basic features of Pascal, including the structure of a Pascal program, procedures, functions, program flow, data types, arrays, records, and pointers. It also tells you how to use many of Pascal's advanced features: dynamic memory management, units, strings, console input/output, and file input/output. Finally, the book shows you how to use both Turbo Pascal and QuickPascal to perform object-oriented programming.

WHAT THIS BOOK WON'T TEACH YOU

This book is not intended to teach you every detail about Turbo Pascal and QuickPascal: that is the job of your compiler reference manuals. Additionally, this book is not intended to teach you a lot of fancy algorithms (methods for problem solving). That type of instruction is better suited for a more general book on advanced programming.

WHAT YOU WILL NEED IN ORDER TO USE THIS BOOK

To use this book, you will need an IBM PC or compatible and either Turbo Pascal or QuickPascal. You will also need a lot of patience and perseverance to become an accomplished Pascal programmer. No matter how well-written this book is, the only way to become a good computer programmer is to write programs, more programs, and even more programs. You'll learn more about programming by successfully tracking down your first bug than I or anyone else could teach you in hours of instruction. Think of this book as a guide. It will get you going in the right direction, but it is up to you to arrive at the proper destination. So if things seem a little hazy at first, stick with it. With a little patience, you'll quickly get the hang of Pascal programming.

Chapter 1

A Simple First Program

T he first step in understanding the Pascal programming language is to become familiar with the components of a Pascal program. Accordingly, this chapter's first lesson acquaints you with all the Pascal programming language's basic and essential components. The chapter concludes with a simple first program.

LESSON 1. The Basic Components of the Pascal Programming Language

This lesson acquaints you with keywords, identifiers, constants, variables, operators, statements, comments, procedures, and functions.

KEYWORDS

All programming languages use a special set of words to perform certain functions. These special words are called **keywords**. Note that some programmers like to refer to keywords as **reserved words**. The terms keywords and reserved words are interchangeable and either is acceptable. Figure 1-1 presents a complete list of the Turbo Pascal keywords, while Figure 1-2 covers the QuickPascal keywords. Because a programming language's keywords all serve a specific purpose, they can never be used in a program for anything other than this intended purpose.

absolute	else	inline	procedure	unit
and	end	interface	program	until
array	external	interrupt	record	uses
begin	file	label	repeat	var
case	for	mod	set	virtual
const	forward	nil	shl	while
constructor	function	not	shr	with
destructor	goto	object	string	xor
div	if	of	then	
do	implementation	or	to	
downto	in	packed	type	

Figure 1-1. The Turbo Pascal keywords.

absolute	end	inline	packed	type
and	external	interface	procedure	unit
array	file	interrupt	program	until
begin	for	label	record	uses
case	forward	mod	repeat	var
const	function	nil	set	while
cstring	goto	not	shl	with
div	if	object	shr	xor
do	implementation	of	string	
downto	in	or	then	
else	inherited	override	to	

Figure 1-2. The QuickPascal keywords.

IDENTIFIERS

As their name implies, identifiers are used to identify something in a Pascal program. For example, program variables, constants, procedures, and functions all require a name. Consequently, each of them is assigned a unique identifier. When constructing an identifier, you must keep the following three rules in mind:

1. An identifier's first character must be either a letter or an underscored character (_).

2. Digits (0, 1, 2, 3, 4, 5, 6, 7, 8, and 9) can be used in an identifier.

3. An identifier can be of any length, but only the first 63 characters of the identifier name are significant.

The following are some examples of valid identifiers:

First_Reading

_last_page

count

b32_45a

_32845

The following are some examples of invalid identifiers. Next to each identifier there is an explanation of how the identifier violates the Pascal identifier rules.

Identifier	Reason For Being Invalid
8times	Starts with a digit.
next loop	Space between next and loop.
name$	$ is an invalid identifier character.
count*three	* is an invalid identifier character.

CONSTANTS

As with all other programming languages, any data found in a Pascal program that never changes its value is called a constant. Constants come in many types (e.g., string, character, real, and integer).

The following are examples of constants:

Constant	Type
Hello	String Constant
'a'	Character Constant
#13	Character Constant
'Another'	String Constant
3.14	Real Constant
12345	Integer Constant
-32.45	Real Constant
456	Integer Constant

The Pascal programming language also permits you to name a constant. Once you assign this name, you can substitute it freely for the constant's value. The following are two examples of named constants:

table_length = 1000;
Authors_Name = 'Mark Goodwin';

VARIABLES

Although constants are a handy tool for the Pascal programmer, variables are even more useful. As its name implies, a variable is a type of data that has a value that can be changed throughout the life of a Pascal program. Unlike constants that can be referred to by their literal values, a variable must always have an identifier name.

OPERATORS

The Pascal operators are a collection of symbols and keywords that are used to build expressions. Figure 1-3 presents a list of these operators. You can use them to perform a wide variety of functions.

Operator	Class
@	Unary
NOT	Boolean
*	Multiplication
/	Multiplication
DIV	Multiplication
MOD	Multiplication
AND	Boolean
SHL	Multiplication
SHR	Multiplication
+	Addition
-	Addition
OR	Boolean
XOR	Boolean
=	Relational
<>	Relational
<	Relational
<=	Relational
>	Relational
>=	Relational
IN	Relational

Figure 1-3. The Pascal operators.

The following are some examples of expressions built from the Pascal operators:

3 + 5 / 2
3 <> 4
3 = 5
32.15 / 3.035

STATEMENTS

A Pascal program statement is a collection of identifiers, keywords, operators, and constants that performs a specific action. The following are some examples of Pascal program statements:

> **name := 'John Doe';**
> **count : integer;**
> **count := 32 * 55;**

As shown above, a Pascal statement ends with a semicolon (;).

Multiple program statements can be defined as a **begin..end** statement block to express a single idea. The following is an example of a block statement:

> **begin**
>> **count := count + 1;**
>> **Writeln(count);**
> **end**

The main body of a Pascal program is nothing more than a **begin..end** statement block.

COMMENTS

A Pascal program comment is exactly what its name implies. It is simply a comment for the programmer's benefit and serves no function as far as the program's execution is concerned. Although they don't affect the program's execution, program comments are a valuable tool for documenting the program. Strategically placed comments clear up things by illustrating a program's inner workings. Many times a program will require modification at a future date. While a program's implementation (a fancy word for how it is written) can seem quite clear when it is originally created, it won't be anywhere near as clear even a week or two down the road. Consequently, comments are one of the Pascal programmer's most valuable tools. You create a Pascal comment by enclosing whatever you want to say in either braces or a (* *) pair.

The following are some examples of Pascal comments:

{ open the file and read in the data }

(* close the file if an error has occurred *)

PROCEDURES AND FUNCTIONS

Two of the most valuable features provided by the Pascal programming language are **procedures** and **functions**. A procedure is a collection of program statements that has been given a name. Essentially it is nothing more than a miniature program. Whenever an executing program encounters a procedure's name, the program branches away from the part of the program it is currently executing and executes the procedure's associated statements. A Pascal function is similar to a procedure except that a function returns a value after its associated statements have been executed. Both procedures and functions can have their own constants and variables.

LESSON 2. A First Program

Now that you know the basic Pascal components, you can write your first Pascal program. This program is presented in Listing 1.1.

Listing 1.1

```
{ first.pas - A first Pascal program }
program First;

const
   number = 3;

var
   count, result : integer;

function multiply(n1, n2 : integer) : integer;
begin
   multiply := n1 * n2;
end;
```
   continued...

```
...from previous page
begin
    count := 2;
    result := count * number;
    Writeln(result);
    result := multiply(count, number);
    Writeln(result);
end.
```

Although Listing 1.1 is fairly short, it serves a very important purpose by illustrating how the Pascal programming language's basic components are brought together in a complete program. To better understand the basic structure of a Pascal program, let's go through the program a line at a time.

{ first.pas - A first Pascal program }
is a comment. It states the program's file name and provides a brief description.

program First;
uses the Pascal keyword **program** to assign the identifier **First** as the program's name. Although assigning a program name isn't absolutely necessary, it is generally considered good programming practice to do so.

const
is the Pascal keyword for defining constants.

number = 3;
assigns the constant value of **3** to the identifier **number**.

var
is the Pascal keyword for defining variable identifiers.

count, result : integer;
defines two variables, **count** and **result**, with type **integer**.

function multiply(n1, n2 : integer) : integer;
defines a function called **multiply**. The function expects two **integer** arguments, **n1** and **n2**, and returns a value of type **integer**.

begin
defines the starting point for the **multiply** function's body.

multiply := n1 * n2;
multiplies the function's arguments and assigns the result as the return value.

end;
defines the end of the **multiply** function's body.

begin
defines the starting point for the program's main body. This is where the program starts executing.

count := 2;
assigns the initial value **2** to the variable **count**.

result := count * number;
multiplies the variable **count** by the constant **number** and assigns the result to the variable **result**.

Writeln(result);
displays the value of **result**.

result := multiply(count, number);
calls the function **multiply,** which simply multiplies **count** by **number**, and assigns the result of the function **call** to the variable **result**.

Writeln(result);
displays the value of **result**.

end.
defines the end of the program's main body. Note that a period—not a semi-colon—follows the **end** keyword. As Lesson 1 stated, a semicolon is used to signify the end of a statement; however, it is always necessary to use a period to signify the end of the program.

Besides showing how the components of the Pascal programming language are used in an actual program, Listing 1.1 also illustrates the use of white space (spaces, tabs, and double spaced lines) to make a program more readable. Note that the use of white space is strictly optional. Nevertheless, it is traditional to write Pascal programs with a fair amount of white space. Without at least a minimal amount of white space, a program will be almost illegible. For example, Listing 1.2 presents the program first.pas (the program that was shown in Listing 1.1) stripped of all of its unnecessary white space. Listing 1.2 is very difficult to read—the version presented in Listing 1.1 is clearly superior.

Listing 1.2

```
{ first.pas - A first Pascal program }program First;const
number = 3;var count, result : integer;function
multiply(n1, n2 : integer) : integer; begin multiply := n1
* n2; end;begin count := 2;result := count * number;
Writeln(result);result := multiply(count,
number);Writeln(result);end.
```

***

You're now familiar with some of the basic components of the Pascal programming language and have examined a simple Pascal program. Chapter 2 discusses predefined data types.

Chapter 2

Predefined Data Types

S ince a Pascal program is called upon to handle many different types of data, the Pascal programming language comes equipped with a rich set of data types. This chapter takes a detailed look at all of these data types, showing how Pascal can satisfy almost any data handling requirements. The data types covered in this chapter include: integers, real numbers, booleans, characters, and strings.

LESSON 3. Integers

Integers are the most basic of the Pascal data types. Simply put, an integer data type can represent whole numbers.

11

The following are examples of integer constants:

32457
-43
0
167
-2335678
$FF

You may be wondering what the constant **$FF** is in the above example. The integer $FF is the way the number 255 is represented using the hexadecimal number system. This number system is base 16 and is represented by the digits **0..9** and the letters **A..F** or **a..f**. Figure 2-1 illustrates how numbers are represented by the hexadecimal number system.

Because the hexadecimal number system is base 16, it's easy to determine that the constant $FF is 255 by performing the following calculation:

$$F * 16 + F = 255 \text{ or } 15 * 16 + 15 = 255$$

Digit	Represents
0	0
1	1
2	2
3	3
4	4
5	5
6	6
7	7
8	8
9	9
A	10
B	11
C	12
D	13
E	14
F	15

Figure 2-1. The hexadecimal number system (base 16).

Because a small whole number, such as the number **2**, doesn't require as much memory to store as a larger whole number, such as the number **356678**, Pascal offers five very distinct integer data types: **ShortInt**, **Byte**, **Integer**, **Word**, and **LongInt**. Figure 2-2 shows the range of numbers these five integer data types can represent.

As figure 2-2 illustrates, a **LongInt** takes two times the amount of memory as an **Integer** and four times the amount of memory as a **ShortInt**. An efficient Pascal programmer will always strive to use the smallest possible data type. For example, an integer variable that will never hold a value less than 0 or greater than 255 should be defined as a **Byte** variable instead of as an **Integer**, **Word**, or **LongInt** variable. Not only do the smaller data types require a great deal less memory than their larger counterparts, the computer can perform operations, such as addition and subtraction, on the smaller data types at much greater speeds.

Figure 2-3 illustrates the format for defining integer variables. As this figure shows, you can define more than one variable per statement by separating the variable identifiers with commas.

Data	Range of Values	Size in Bytes
ShortInt	-128 to 127	1
Byte	0 to 255	1
Integer	-32768 to 32767	2
Word	0 to 65535	2
LongInt	-2147483648 to 2147483647	4

Figure 2-2. The Pascal integer types.

```
var
        identifier : integer data type;
        identifier, identifier : integer data type;


Where:
        identifier                      is the variable's name.

        integer data type               is ShortInt, Byte, Integer,
                                        Word, or LongInt.
```

Figure 2-3. Defining an integer variable.

Are these literals?
Maybe they mean — shown in
constants such as example ppm
120 on pg 7.

The following examples illustrate integer variable definitions:

number : Integer;
small_number : Byte;
offset : Word;
AccountNumber, AccountBalance : LongInt;

In addition to named constants, the Pascal programming language also supports typed constants. Although the value of a Pascal named constant never changes, a typed constant's value can be changed. Basically, a typed constant functions as a variable with an initial value. Figure 2-4 illustrates the structure for defining integer constants. Unlike variable definitions, you can only define one constant per definition statement.

The following examples illustrate typed integer constant definitions:

top_row : Integer = 0;
bottom_row : Integer = 24;
left_column : Byte = 0;
right_column : Byte = 79;
CashAccount : LongInt = 100000;

Listing 2.1 illustrates the use of Pascal's integer data types. It presents a short program that defines a number of integer variables and constants and displays their assigned values.

---

const
    identifier : integer data type = constant;

Where:
    identifier   is the constant's name.

    integer data type   is **ShortInt, Byte, Integer, Word,** or **LongInt.**

    constant   is a constant value or expression.

Figure 2-4. Defining a typed integer constant.

Listing 2.1

```pascal
{ list2-1.pas - Define and display a variety of integers }
program integers;

const
      short_const : shortint = -1;
      byte_const : byte = $3E;
      integer_const : integer = 3245;
      word_const : word = 45667;
      longint_const : longint = 1000000;

var
      short_var : shortint;
      byte_var : byte;
      integer_var : integer;
      word_var : word;
      longint_var : longint;

begin
      short_var := 22;
      byte_var := 254;
      integer_var := -5563;
      word_var := $2224;
      longint_var := -32;
      writeln('short_const    = ', short_const);
      writeln('byte_const     = ', byte_const);
      writeln('integer_const = ', integer_const);
      writeln('word_const     = ', word_const);
      writeln('longint_const = ', longint_const);
      writeln('short_var      = ', short_var);
      writeln('byte_var       = ', byte_var);
      writeln('integer_var   = ', integer_var);
      writeln('word_var       = ', word_var);
      writeln('longint_var   = ', longint_var);
end.
```

LESSON 4.   Real Numbers

Although Pascal's integer types are quite useful and can meet the needs of a wide variety of numeric data, many types of numeric data require a fractional part to maintain a high degree of accuracy. Real numbers meet this requirement. The following are some examples of real numbers:

> -32.36789
> 1.5E+2
> .000000056789
> 55.67
> -25.3999999
> .333333333

In order to represent real numbers efficiently, Pascal offers five different real number types: **Single**, **Real** (or floating point), **Double**, **Extended**, and **Comp**. The **Comp** data type is unique. It is used to store extremely large integers and doesn't save a number's fractional part. Figure 2-5 illustrates the range of numbers that the five real number data types can represent.

As with the integer types, Pascal's real number types take a varying amount of memory to store. Consequently, you should always try to use the smallest real number type possible for a given task. As with integer types, calculations are performed much faster on the smaller real number types than on the larger real number types.

Figure 2-6 shows the format for defining real number variables. As this figure illustrates, you can define more than one variable per statement by separating the variable identifiers with commas.

Data Type	Range of Values	Size in Bytes	Significant Data
Single	1.5E-45 to 3.4E+38	4	7-8
Real	2.9E-39 to 1.7E+38	6	11-12
Double	5.0E-324 to 1.7E+308	8	15-16
Extended	3.4E-4951 to 1.1E+4932	10	15-16
Comp	-9.2E+18 to 9.2E+18	8	15-16

Figure 2-5. The Pascal real number types.

```
    var
            identifier : real number data type;
            identifier, identifier : real number data type;

    Where:
            identifier                    is the variable's name.

            real number data type    is Single, Real, Double, Extended, or
                                      Comp.
```

Figure 2-6. Defining a real number variable.

The following examples illustrate real number variable definitions:

AccountBalance : Double;
degrees : Single;
Population : Comp;
CityBudget : Extended;
Credit, Debit : Real;

As it does with their integer counterparts, Pascal supports typed real number constants. Figure 2-7 shows the format for defining typed real number constants. As with typed integer constants, you can only define one constant per definition statement.

```
    constant  ← should this be "const" ?
            indentifier : real number data type = constant;

    Where:
            identifier                    is the constant's name.

            real number data type    is Single, Real, Double, Extended, or
                                      Comp.
```

Figure 2-7. Defining a typed real number constant.

17

The following examples illustrate real number typed constant definitions:

CashAccount : Double = -456.37;
WallHeight : Single = 32.33678;
degrees : Extended = .000000678;

Listing 2.2 illustrates the use of Pascal's real number data types. It presents a brief program that defines a number of real number variables and constants and displays their assigned values.

Listing 2.2

```
{ list2-2.pas - Define and display a variety of real numbers }
program real_numbers;

{$E+} { Turbo Pascal 8087 Emulation Directive - Omit For
      QuickPascal }
{$N+} { Turbo Pascal 8087 Directive - Omit For QuickPascal }

const
    single_const : single = 32.3;
    real_const : real = -0.0000032;
    double_const : double = 666.788888;
    extended_const : extended = 999.999;
    comp_const : comp = 32456789;

var
    single_var : single;
    real_var : real;
    double_var : double;
    extended_var : extended;
    comp_var : comp;

begin
    single_var := -45.667;
    real_var := 32.4568;
    double_var := 10000.34;
```
continued...

18

...from previous page
```
      extended_var := 55000.0003;
      comp_var := -4567;
      writeln('single_const   = ', single_const);
      writeln('real_const     = ', real_const);
      writeln('double_const   = ', double_const);
      writeln('extended_const = ', extended_const);
      writeln('comp_cont      = ', comp_const);
      writeln('single_var     = ', single_var);
      writeln('real_var       = ', real_var);
      writeln('double_var     = ', double_var);
      writeln('extended_var   = ', extended_var);
      writeln('comp_var       = ', comp_var);
end.
```

LESSON 5. Booleans

Many expressions in a computer program will return either a **True** or **False** result. Unlike most other programming languages, Pascal provides a data type just for handling **True/False** values. This predefined data type is known as the **Boolean** data type. Because it represents only two logical values (**True** or **False**) the **boolean** data type will always hold either a **True** or a **False** value.

Figure 2-8 shows the format for defining boolean variables. As this figure illustrates, you can define more than one variable per statement by separating the variable identifiers with commas.

---

var
         identifier : **Boolean;**
         identifier, identifier : **Boolean;**

Where:
         identifier   is the variable's name.

Figure 2-8. Defining a boolean variable.

The following examples illustrate boolean variable definitions:

Flag : Boolean;
IOResult : Boolean;
answer1, answer2 : Boolean;
On_Off_Flag : Boolean;
Error_Flag : Boolean;

As with integers and real numbers, typed boolean constants can be defined with Pascal. Figure 2-9 defines how typed boolean constants are defined. Like other typed constants, you can only define one typed boolean constant per definition statement.

The following examples illustrate typed boolean constant definitions:

ARE "FALSE" and "TRUE" pre-understood by PASCAL?

Flag : Boolean = False;
True_Result : Boolean = True;
Not_On : Boolean = False;

Listing 2.3 demonstrates the use of Pascal's boolean data type. It presents a brief program that defines a number of boolean variables and constants and displays their assigned values.

const
      identifier : **Boolean** = constant;

Where:
      identifier   is the constant's name.

      constant   is a constant value or expression.

Figure 2-9. Defining a typed boolean constant.

Listing 2.3

```
{ list2-3.pas - Define and display a variety of booleans }
program booleans;

const
      false_flag : boolean = false;
      not_on_flag : boolean = false;

var
      flag : boolean;
      ioresult : boolean;

begin
      flag := false;
      ioresult := true;
      writeln('false_flag  = ', false_flag);
      writeln('not_on_flag = ', not_on_flag);
      writeln('flag        = ', flag);
      writeln('ioresult    = ', ioresult);
end.
```

LESSON 6. Characters — *is this always 1 character long ?*

Quite often the result of an action will be a character of data. The following are
some examples of actions that result in characters:

> **keyboard input**
> **display output**
> **printer output**
> **some forms of disk input/output**

Pascal offers the **Char** data type to properly deal with character data. Figure 2-10
defines the three forms of valid Pascal character data.

Type	Representation
Control Characters	are represented with the carat symbol (^) followed by a control letter. For example, the control character 1 is represented by **^A**, the control character 2 is represented by **^B**, etc.
Readable Characters	are represented in the form "character." For example the letter **a** is represented by "**a**."
All Characters	are represented with the number sign (#) followed by the character's ASCII code number. For example, the letter **g** is represented by **#103**.

Where:

Control Characters	are the ASCII characters 0 through 31.
Readable Characters	are the alphabetic, numeric, and punctuation characters.
All Characters	are any character in the ASCII code table.

Figure 2-10. Pascal character data representations.

The following are some examples of character data:

^M
#255
'k'
'y'
#10

Figure 2-11 shows the format for defining character variables. As this figure illustrates, you can define more than one variable per statement by separating the variable identifiers with commas.

```
var
        identifier : Char
        identifier, identifier : Char

Where:
        identifier                      is the variable's name.
```

Figure 2-11. Defining a character variable.

The following examples illustrate character variable definitions:

Key : Char;
ReturnCode : Char;
First_Initial, Middle_Initial : Char;
DiskIO : Char;
PrinterCode : Char;

As it does with other data types, Pascal supports typed character constants. Figure 2-12 illustrates the format for defining typed character constants. As with other typed constants, you can only define one constant per definition statement.

The following examples illustrate typed character constant definitions:

CR : Char = ^M;
PrinterCode : Char = 'B';
LF : Char = #10;
ErrorCode : Char = 'E';

```
const
        identifier : Char = constant;

Where:
        identifier                      is the constant's name.
```

Figure 2-12. Defining a typed character constant.

Listing 2.4 demonstrates the use of Pascal's character data type in a program that defines a number of character variables and constants and displays their assigned values.

Listing 2.4

```
{ list2-4.pas - Define and display a variety of characters }
program characters;

const
    CR : char = ^M;
    LF : char = #10;

var
   a_character : char;
   another_character : char;

begin
    a_character := 'a';
    another_character := 'b';
    writeln('CR                   = ', CR);
    writeln('LF                   = ', LF);
    writeln('a_character          = ', a_character);
    writeln('another_character = ', another_character);
end.
```

LESSON 7.   Strings

Although all of the previously described Pascal data types are important, string data is perhaps the most important data a Pascal program handles. From word processing programs to simple utility programs, strings are by far the most prevalent type of computer data. Pascal offers the **String** data type to meet the needs that string handling imposes upon a computer language. The examples listed at the top of the opposite page are string data.

'This is a sample string'
'This is another sample string'
'This a more complex'#13#10'string.'
'I''m a string, too!'

↳ *double apostrophe, not quote.*

Note the use of the double apostrophe (") in the last example. Because Pascal strings are delimited (a fancy word for surrounded) by apostrophes, you must use a double apostrophe to signify an apostrophe inside of a string. Failure to use a double apostrophe will confuse the compiler into thinking the string is much shorter than it should be.

Figure 2-13 shows the format for defining string variables. As this figure indicates, you can define more than one variable per statement by separating the variable identifiers with commas. The figure also shows that an optional length of up to 255 characters can be specified for a string.

The following examples illustrate string variable definitions:

Name : String[30];
City, State, Zip : String;
DisplayLine : String[80];
Address : String[30];
Response : String;

---

var
       identifier : **String;**
       identifier : **String** [length];
       identifier, identifier : **String;**
       identifier, identifier : **String**[length];

Where:
       identifier   is the variable's name.

       length   is the string's length, which
                              must be in the range of 1 to 255.

Figure 2-13. Defining a string variable.

As it does with the other data types, Pascal supports typed string constants. Figure 2-14 illustrates the format for defining typed string constants. As with other typed constants, you can only define one typed string constant per definition statement.

---

const

       identifier : **String** = constant;
       identifier : **String** [length] = constant;

Where:

identifier	is the constant's name.
constant	is a constant value or expression.
length	is the string's maximum length, which must be in the range of 1 to 255.

Figure 2-14. Defining a typed string constant.

The following examples illustrate typed string constant definitions:

name : String = 'Jane Smith';
city : String[30] = 'Los Angeles';
State : String[2] = 'NV';
zipcode : String = '05501';

Listing 2.5 demonstrates the use of Pascal's string data type. It presents a brief program that defines a number of character variables and constants and displays their assigned values.

Listing 2.5

```
{ list2-5.pas - Define and display a variety of strings }
program strings;

const
     name : string[20] = 'John Doe';
     city : string = 'Boston';
```
continued...

...from previous page

```
var
      state : string;
      ZipCode : string[5];

begin
      state := 'MA';
      ZipCode := '00001';
      writeln('name    = ', name);
      writeln('city    = ', city);
      writeln('state   = ', state);
      writeln('ZipCode = ', ZipCode);
end.
```

***

You're now familiar with predefined data types: integers, real numbers, booleans, characters, and strings. Chapter 3 discusses how you can use Pascal operators to manipulate data.

Chapter 3

The Pascal Operators

This chapter shows you how to use the Pascal operators to manipulate data. When combined with other variables and constants, the Pascal operators—assignment, multiplication, bitwise, and string concatenation—can be used to build powerful and useful expressions. The chapter concludes with a discussion of operator precedence.

LESSON 8. The Assignment Operator

As its name implies, the Pascal assignment operator (:=) assigns the result of an expression to a variable or typed constant. Because of its extensive use in the programs listed in Chapter 2, you should already be somewhat familiar with the assignment operator. Figure 3-1 defines the assignment operator.

```
identifier := expression
```

Where:

    identifier   is a variable or typed constant name.

    expression   is a valid Pascal expression.

Figure 3-1. The Pascal assignment operator.

The following examples illustrate the proper use of the assignment operator:

**flag := False;
count := count + 1;
key := ReadKey;
Name := FirstName + ' ' + MiddleInitial + ' ' + LastName;
pi := 22 / 7;**

Listing 3.1 demonstrates how the Pascal assignment operator is used in an actual program that assigns values to a wide variety of variables.

Listing 3.1

```
{ list3-1.pas - Demonstrate the use of the Pascal
assignment operator }
program assignment_operator;

var
      count, number : integer;
      flag : boolean;
      Name : string;

begin
      count := 1;
      count := count + 1;
      flag := False;
continued...
```

...from previous page
```
      Name := 'John' + ' ' + 'Q. ' + 'Public';
      writeln('count = ', count);
      writeln('flag  = ', flag);
      writeln('Name  = ', Name);
end.
```

LESSON 9.   The Unary Plus Operator

The Pascal unary plus operator (+) simply maintains the sign of an expression. In other words, it doesn't do a thing. This may seem to be a ludicrous statement, but it's quite true. The unary plus operator is ignored by Pascal and is only included in the language definition to prevent the compiler from generating unnecessary syntax errors. Figure 3-2 defines the unary plus operator.

+expression

Where:

       expression   is a valid Pascal expression.

Figure 3-2. The Pascal unary plus operator.

The following examples illustrate the proper use of the unary plus operator:

    +count
    +1.234
    +recordnumber

Listing 3.2 demonstrates how the Pascal unary plus operator is used in an actual program.

Listing 3.2

```
{ list3-2.pas - Demonstrate the use of the Pascal unary
plus operator }
program unary_plus_operator;
```
continued...

...from previous page

```
var
      n1, n2 : integer;
      r1 : real;

begin
      r1 := +32.333;
      n1 := -23;
      n2 := +n1;
      writeln('n1 = ', n1);
      writeln('n2 = ', n2);
      writeln('r1 = ', r1);
end.
```

LESSON 10. The Unary Minus Operator

The Pascal unary minus operator (-) negates the value of an expression. If the expression is negative, the unary minus operator makes it positive. If the expression is positive, the unary minus operator makes it negative. Figure 3-3 defines the unary minus operator.

The following examples illustrate the proper use of the unary minus operator:

-n1
-2.345678
-count

Listing 3.3 demonstrates how the Pascal unary minus operator is used in an actual program.

-expression

Where:
     expression   is a valid Pascal expression.

Figure 3-3. The Pascal unary minus operator.

Listing 3.3

```
{ list3-3.pas - Demonstrate the use of the Pascal unary
minus operator }
program unary_minus_operator;

var
      n1, n2 : integer;
      r1 : real;

begin
      r1 := -32.333;
      n1 := -23;
      n2 := -n1;
      writeln('n1 = ', n1);
      writeln('n2 = ', n2);
      writeln('r1 = ', r1);
end.
```

LESSON 11. The Addition Operator

The Pascal addition operator (+) adds together two expressions. Figure 3-4 defines the addition operator.

The following examples illustrate the proper use of the addition operator:

1 + 1
n1 + 3
33.333 + 500
22 + n2
i + j

---

expression + expression

Where:
        expression   is a valid Pascal expression.

Figure 3-4. The Pascal addition operator.

Listing 3.4 demonstrates how the Pascal addition operator is used in an actual program.

Listing 3.4

```
{ list3-4.pas - Demonstrate the use of the Pascal addition operator }
program addition_operator;

var
      n1, n2 : integer;
      r1 : real;

begin
      r1 := -32.4567 + 33 + 0.67;
      n1 := 1 + 45;
      n2 := n1 + 1;
      writeln('n1 = ', n1);
      writeln('n2 = ', n2);
      writeln('r1 = ', r1);
end.
```

LESSON 12. The Subtraction Operator

The Pascal subtraction operator (-) subtracts the result of one expression from the result of another expression. Figure 3-5 defines the subtraction operator.

The following examples illustrate the proper use of the subtraction operator:

2 - 3
33.456 - 1.325
n1 - g - c
55 - n1 - 3
6 - 1

---

expression - expression

Where:
      expression   is a valid Pascal expression.

Figure 3-5. The Pascal subtraction operator.

Listing 3.5 demonstrates how the Pascal subtraction operator is used in an actual program.

Listing 3.5

```
{ list3-5.pas - Demonstrate the use of the Pascal
subtraction operator }
program subtraction_operator;

var
     n1, n2 : integer;
     r1 : real;

begin
     r1 := 32.4567 - 33 - 0.67;
     n1 := 1 - 45;
     n2 := n1 - 1;
     writeln('n1 = ', n1);
     writeln('n2 = ', n2);
     writeln('r1 = ', r1);
end.
```

LESSON 13. The Multiplication Operator

The Pascal multiplication operator (*) multiplies the result of one expression by the result of another expression. Figure 3-6 defines the multiplication operator.

expression * expression

Where:
        expression   is a valid Pascal expression.

Figure 3-6. The Pascal multiplication operator.

The following examples illustrate the proper use of the multiplication operator:

3 * 4
n * pi
3.43 * 0.5
99 * 6
x * y * z

Listing 3.6 demonstrates how the Pascal multiplication operator is used in an actual program.

Listing 3.6

```
{ list3-6.pas - Demonstrate the use of the Pascal
multiplication operator }
program multiplication_operator;

var
      n1, n2 : integer;
      r1 : real;

begin
      r1 := 32.4567 * 27 * 0.5;
      n1 := 1 * 45;
      n2 := n1 * n1;
      writeln('n1 = ', n1);
      writeln('n2 = ', n2);
      writeln('r1 = ', r1);
end.
```

LESSON 14. The Real Number Division Operator

The Pascal real number division operator (/) divides the result of one expression by the result of another expression. As you will soon see, the Pascal division operators are unique. All of the previously covered arithmetic operators (+, -, and *) return the same data type as the expressions to which they are applied. For example, the addition of two integer expressions returns an integer result. The real number division operator differs from the other arithmetic operators by always returning a real number result. It doesn't matter whether the expressions being divided are integers or real numbers; the calculated result is always returned as a real number. Figure 3-7 defines the real number division operator.

---

expression / expression

Where:
        expression   is a valid Pascal expression.

Figure 3-7. The Pascal real number operator.

The following examples illustrate the proper use of the real number division operator:

22 / 7
15 / n1
x / z / y
count / 2
15.333 / 2.1023

Listing 3.7 demonstrates how the Pascal real number division operator is used in an actual program.

Listing 3.7

```
{ list3-7.pas - Demonstrate the use of the Pascal real
number division operator }
program division_operator;

var
     r1 : real;

begin
     r1 := 32.4567 / 27 / 0.5;
     writeln('r1 = ', r1);
end.
```

LESSON 15. The Integer Division Operator

The Pascal integer division operator (**div**) divides the result of one integer expression by the result of another integer expression. The integer division operator always returns an integer result. Figure 3-8 defines the integer division operator.

---

integer expression **div** integer expression

Where:
    integer expression   is a valid Pascal integer expression.

Figure 3-8. The Pascal integer division operator.

The following examples illustrate the proper use of the integer division operator:

22 div 7
n div 3
x div y div 2
16 div 8
5555 div n1

Listing 3.8 demonstrates how the Pascal integer division operator is used in an actual program.

Listing 3.8

```
{ list3-8.pas - Demonstrate the use of the Pascal integer
division operator }
program integer_division_operator;

var
      n1, n2 : integer;

begin
      n1 := 3400 div 16;
      n2 := n1 div 3;
      writeln('n1 = ', n1);
      writeln('n2 = ', n2);
end.
```

LESSON 16. The Remainder Operator

The Pascal remainder operator (**mod**) calculates a remainder by dividing the result of one integer expression by the result of another integer expression. The remainder operator always returns an integer result. Figure 3-9 defines the remainder operator.

---

integer expression **mod** integer expression

Where:
>   integer expression   is a valid Pascal integer expression.

Figure 3-9. The Pascal remainder operator.

The following examples illustrate the proper use of the remainder operator:

> **count mod 5**
> **33 mod 2**
> **45 mod n**
> **x mod y mod z**
> **n1 mod n2**

Listing 3.9 demonstrates how the Pascal remainder operator is used in an actual program.

Listing 3.9

```
{ list3-9.pas - Demonstrate the use of the Pascal
remainder operator }
program remainder_operator;

var
     n1, n2 : integer;

begin
     n1 := 3400 mod 16;
     n2 := n1 mod 3;
```
continued...

...from previous page
```
      writeln('n1 = ', n1);
      writeln('n2 = ', n2);
end.
```

LESSON 17. The Logical Negation Operator

The Pascal logical negation operator (**not**) negates the result of a boolean expression. If the boolean expression is equal to **True**, the logical negation operator makes it **False**. If the boolean expression is equal to **False**, the logical negation operator makes it **True**.

Figure 3-10 presents a truth table that illustrates how the logical negation operator performs its function. Figure 3-11 defines the logical negation operator.

The following examples illustrate the proper use of the logical negation operator:

> **not flag**
> **not False**
> **not error_flag**

Value X	Value Y	Result not X
True		True
False		False

Figure 3-10. A logical negation truth table.

not boolean expression

Where:
> boolean expression   is a valid Pascal boolean expression.

Figure 3-11. The Pascal logical negation operator.

Listing 3.10 illustrates how the Pascal logical negation operator is used in an actual program that displays a logical negation truth table.

Listing 3.10

```
{ list3-10.pas - Demonstrate the Pascal logical negation
operator }
program logical_negation_operator;

begin
     writeln('Logical Negation Truth Table');
     writeln('=============================');
     writeln('Value     Value      Result');
     writeln('X                    Not X');
     writeln('----------------------------');
     writeln('True               ', not True);
     writeln('False              ', not False);
     writeln('===========================');
end.
```

LESSON 18. The Logical and Operator

The Pascal logical and operator (**and**) compares two boolean expressions and returns a **True** result only if both of the boolean expressions are equal to **True**. Otherwise, the logical and operator returns a **False** result.

Figure 3-12 presents a truth table that illustrates how the logical and operator performs its function. Figure 3-13 defines the logical and operator.

Value X	Value Y	Result X and Y
True	True	True
True	False	False
False	True	False
False	False	False

Figure 3-12. A logical and truth table.

> boolean expression **and** boolean expression
>
> **Where:**
>
> boolean expression   is a valid Pascal boolean expression.

Figure 3-13. The Pascal logical and operator.

The following examples illustrate the proper use of the logical and operator:

flag and True
error and EndOfFile
keypressed and flag

Listing 3.11 demonstrates how the Pascal logical and operator is used in an actual program that displays a logical and truth table.

Listing 3.11

```
{ list3-11.pas - Demonstrate the Pascal logical and
operator }
program logical_and_operator;

begin
      writeln('Logical And Truth Table');
      writeln('=============================');
      writeln('Value     Value     Result');
      writeln('X         Y         X AND Y');
      writeln('-----------------------------');
      writeln('True      True      ', True and True);
      writeln('True      False     ', True and False);
      writeln('False     True      ', False and True);
      writeln('False     False     ', False and False);
      writeln('=============================');
end.
```

LESSON 19. The Logical or Operator

The Pascal logical or operator (**or**) compares two boolean expressions and returns a **True** result if either of the boolean expressions is equal to **True**. The logical or operator returns a **False** result only if both boolean expressions are equal to **False**.

Figure 3-14 presents a truth table that illustrates how the logical or operator performs its function. Figure 3-15 defines the use of the logical or operator.

The following examples illustrate the proper use of the logical or operator:

flag or True
error or EndOfFile
keypressed or mouseclicked

Listing 3.12 illustrates how the Pascal logical or operator is used in an **actual** program that displays a logical or truth table.

Value X	Value Y	Result X or Y
True	True	True
True	False	True
False	True	True
False	False	False

Figure 3-14. A logical or truth table.

boolean expression **or** boolean expression

Where:

      boolean expression   is a valid Pascal boolean expression.

Figure 3-15 . The Pascal logical or operator.

Listing 3.12

```
{ list3-12.pas - Demonstrate the Pascal logical or
operator }
program logical_or_operator;

begin
    writeln('Logical Or Truth Table');
    writeln('=============================');
    writeln('Value     Value      Result');
    writeln('X         Y          X OR Y');
    writeln('----------------------------');
    writeln('True      True       ', True or True);
    writeln('True      False      ', True or False);
    writeln('False     True       ', False or True);
    writeln('False     False      ', False or False);
    writeln('=============================');

end.
```

LESSON 20. The Exclusive or Operator

The Pascal exclusive or operator (**xor**) compares two boolean expressions and returns a **True** result if both of the boolean expressions are different. Otherwise, the exclusive or operator returns a **False** result.

Figure 3-16 presents a truth table that illustrates how the exclusive or operator performs its function. Figure 3-17 defines the exclusive or operator.

Value X	Value Y	Result X or Y
True	True	False
True	False	True
False	True	True
False	False	False

Figure 3-16. An exclusive or truth table.

44

---

boolean expression **xor** boolean expression ·

Where:
      boolean expression   is a valid Pascal boolean expression.

Figure 3-17. The Pascal exclusive or operator.

The following examples illustrate the proper use of the exclusive or operator:

flag xor True
error xor False
keypressed xor mouseclicked

Listing 3.13 demonstrates how the Pascal exclusive or operator is used in an actual program that displays an exclusive or truth table.

Listing 3.13

```
{ list3-13.pas - Demonstrate the Pascal exclusive or
operator }
program exclusive_or_operator;

begin
     writeln('Exclusive Or Truth Table');
     writeln('=============================');
     writeln('Value     Value      Result');
     writeln('X         Y          X XOR Y');
     writeln('-----------------------------');
     writeln('True      True       ', True xor True);
     writeln('True      False      ', True xor False);
     writeln('False     True       ', False xor True);
     writeln('False     False      ', False xor False);
     writeln('=============================');
end.
```

LESSON 21. The Bitwise Negation Operator

The Pascal bitwise negation operator (**not**) negates the result of an integer expression. The bitwise negation operator performs its intended function by inverting the value of each of an integer's **bits**. If you are unfamiliar with the term bit, Figure 3-18 should be of assistance. As this figure illustrates, each byte of memory (one character of memory) is comprised of eight bits. Each bit holds the value of either 1 or 0. By simply inverting each of the integer expression's bits, the bitwise negation operator effectively negates the expression.

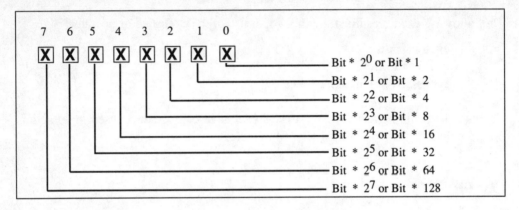

Figure 3-18. A byte of bits.

Figure 3-19 presents a truth table that illustrates how the bitwise negation operator performs its function. Figure 3-20 defines the bitwise negation operator.

Bit Value X	Bit Value	Result not X
1		0
0		1

Figure 3-19. A bitwise negation truth table.

---

not integer expression

Where:
    integer expression   is a valid Pascal integer expression.

Figure 3-20. The Pascal bitwise negation operator.

The following examples illustrate the proper use of the bitwise negation operator:

> **not mask**
> **not pixels**
> **not bit_mask**

Listing 3.14 demonstrates how the Pascal bitwise negation operator is used in an actual program that displays a bitwise negation truth table.

Listing 3.14

```
{ list3-14.pas - Demonstrate the Pascal bitwise negation
operator }
program bitwise_negation_operator;

const
      one = not 0;
      zero = not 1;

begin
      writeln('Bitwise Negation Truth Table');
      writeln('============================');
      writeln('Value     Value     Result');
      writeln('X                   not X');
      writeln('---------------------------');
      writeln('1                   ', not one);
      writeln('0                   ', not zero);
      writeln('---------------------------');
end.
```

LESSON 22. The Bitwise and Operator

The Pascal bitwise and operator (**and**) compares two integer expressions and returns the result of performing **and** operations on them bit-by-bit.

Figure 3-21 presents a truth table that illustrates how the bitwise and operator performs its function. Figure 3-22 defines the bitwise and operator.

The following examples illustrate the proper use of the bitwise and operator:

value and BitMask
ShiftPressed and 1
Pixels and $F0

Listing 3.15 demonstrates how the Pascal bitwise and operator is used in an actual program that displays a bitwise and truth table.

Bit Value X	Bit Value Y	Result X and Y
1	1	1
1	0	0
0	1	0
0	0	0

Figure 3-21. A bitwise and truth table.

integer expression **and** integer expression

Where:

integer expression   is a valid Pascal integer expression.

Figure 3-22. The Pascal bitwise and operator.

Listing 3.15

```
{ list3-15.pas - Demonstrate the Pascal bitwise and
operator }
program bitwise_and_operator;

begin
    writeln('Bitwise And Truth Table');
    writeln('=============================');
    writeln('Value     Value       Result');
    writeln('X         Y           X and Y');
    writeln('----------------------------');
    writeln('1         1           ', 1 and 1);
    writeln('1         0           ', 1 and 0);
    writeln('0         1           ', 0 and 1);
    writeln('0         0           ', 0 and 0);
    writeln('----------------------------');
end.
```

LESSON 23. The Bitwise or Operator

The Pascal bitwise or operator (**or**) compares two integer expressions and returns the result of performing **or** operations on them bit-by-bit.

Figure 3-23 presents a truth table that illustrates how the bitwise or operator performs its function. Figure 3-24 defines the bitwise or operator.

Bit Value X	Bit Value Y	Result X or Y
1	1	1
1	0	1
0	1	1
0	0	0

Figure 3-23. A bitwise or truth table.

---

integer expression **or** integer expression

Where:

        integer expression   is a valid Pascal integer expression.

Figure 3-24. The Pascal bitwise or operator.

The following examples illustrate the proper use of the bitwise or operator:

pixel or 1
flags or mask
shiftmask or 2

Listing 3.16 demonstrates how the Pascal bitwise or operator is used in an actual program that displays a bitwise or truth table.

Listing 3.16

```
{ list3-16.pas - Demonstrate the Pascal bitwise or
operator }
program bitwise_or_operator;

begin
     writeln('Bitwise Or Truth Table');
     writeln('==============================');
     writeln('Value     Value      Result');
     writeln('X         Y          X or Y');
     writeln('----------------------------');
     writeln('1         1          ', 1 or 1);
     writeln('1         0          ', 1 or 0);
     writeln('0         1          ', 0 or 1);
     writeln('0         0          ', 0 or 0);
     writeln('----------------------------');
end.
```

LESSON 24. The Bitwise Exclusive or Operator

The Pascal bitwise exclusive or operator (**xor**) compares two integer expressions and returns the result of performing xor functions on them bit-by-bit.

Figure 3-25 presents a truth table that illustrates how the bitwise exclusive or operator performs its function. Figure 3-26 defines the bitwise exclusive or operator.

The following examples illustrate the proper use of the bitwise exclusive or operator:

> **pixels xor $FF**
> **ErrorFlag xor mask**
> **ShiftFlag xor 1**

Listing 3.17 demonstrates how the Pascal bitwise exclusive or operator is used in an actual program that displays a bitwise exclusive or truth table.

Bit Value X	Bit Value Y	Result X xor Y
1	1	0
1	0	1
0	1	1
0	0	0

Figure 3-25. A bitwise exclusive or truth table.

integer expression **xor** integer expression

Where:
>   integer expression   is a valid Pascal integer expression.

Figure 3-26. The Pascal bitwise exclusive or operator.

Listing 3.17

```
{ list3-17.pas - Demonstrate the Pascal bitwise xor
operator }
program bitwise_xor_operator;

begin
    writeln('Bitwise Xor Truth Table');
    writeln('==============================');
    writeln('Value      Value       Result');
    writeln('X          Y           X xor Y');
    writeln('----------------------------');
    writeln('1          1          ', 1 xor 1);
    writeln('1          0          ', 1 xor 0);
    writeln('0          1          ', 0 xor 1);
    writeln('0          0          ', 0 xor 0);
    writeln('----------------------------');
end.
```

LESSON 25. The Bitwise Shift Left Operator

The Pascal bitwise shift left operator (**shl**) shifts all of the bits in an integer expression to the left by the number of places specified by another integer expression. Essentially, the shift left operator multiplies an integer value two times for every position to the left it is shifted. For example, the expression **4 shl 2** has the same effect as the expression **4 * 4**.

Figure 3-27 defines the shift left operator.

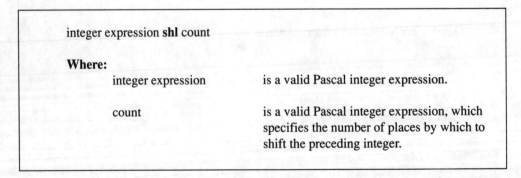

integer expression **shl** count

Where:

integer expression	is a valid Pascal integer expression.
count	is a valid Pascal integer expression, which specifies the number of places by which to shift the preceding integer.

Figure 3-27. The Pascal shift left operator.

The following examples illustrate the proper use of the shift left operator:

> **mask shl 1**
> **number shl count**
> **4 shl count**

Listing 3.18 demonstrates how the Pascal shift left operator is used in an actual program.

Listing 3.18

```
{ list3-18.pas - Demonstrate the Pascal bitwise shift left
operator }
program bitwise_shift_left_operator;

var
      n1, n2 : integer;

begin
      n1 := 4 shl 1;
      n2 := n1 shl 2;
      writeln('n1 = ', n1);
      writeln('n2 = ', n2);
end.
```

LESSON 26. The Bitwise Shift Right Operator

The Pascal bitwise shift right operator (**shr**) shifts all of the bits in an integer expression to the right by the number of places specified by another integer expression. Essentially, the shift right operator divides an integer value two times for every position to the right it is shifted. For example, the expression **63 shr 1** has the same effect as the expression **63 div 2**.

Figure 3-28 defines the shift right operator.

---

integer expression **shr** count

Where:

integer expression	is a valid Pascal integer expression.
count	is a valid Pascal integer expression, which specifies the number of places by which to shift the preceding integer.

Figure 3-28. The Pascal shift right operator.

The following examples illustrate the proper use of the shift right operator:

mask shr 2
number shr count
45 shr times

Listing 3.19 demonstrates how the Pascal shift right operator is used in an actual program.

Listing 3.19

```
{ list3-19.pas - Demonstrate the Pascal bitwise shift
right operator }
program bitwise_shift_right_operator;

var
      n1, n2 : integer;

begin
      n1 := 64 shr 1;
      n2 := n1 shr 2;
      writeln('n1 = ', n1);
      writeln('n2 = ', n2);
end.
```

LESSON 27. The String Concatenation Operator

The Pascal string concatenation operator (+) is used to combine characters and strings to form an even larger string. Figure 3.29 defines the string concatenation operator.

---

string expression + string expression
string expression + character expression
character expression + string expression
character expression + character expression

Where:

    string expression   is a valid Pascal string expression.

    character expression   is a valid Pascal character
                             expression.

Figure 3-29. The Pascal string concatenation operator.

The following examples illustrate the proper use of the string concatenation operator:

    'Washington' + 'D.C.'
    #13 + String
    FirstName + MiddleInitial + LastName

Listing 3.20 demonstrates how the Pascal string concatenation operator is used in an actual program.

Listing 3.20

```
{ list3-20.pas - Demonstrate the Pascal string
concatenation operator }
program string_concatenation_operator;

var
     FirstName, Lastname, Name : string;
     MiddleInitial : char;
continued...
```

...from previous page

```
begin
      FirstName := 'John';
      LastName := 'Smith';
      MiddleInitial := 'D';
      Name := FirstName + #32 + MiddleInitial + '. ' + LastName;
      writeln('Name = ', Name);
end.
```

LESSON 28. The Equal to Operator

The Pascal equal to operator (=) compares two expressions to see if they are equal in value. If the two expressions are equal, the equal to operator returns a value of **True**. If the two expressions aren't equal, the equal to operator returns a value of **False**. Figure 3-30 defines the equal to operator.

The following examples illustrate the proper use of the equal to operator:

> **Flag = True**
> **n = 1**
> **15.0 = Diameter**

Listing 3.21 demonstrates how the Pascal equal to operator is used in an actual program.

---

expression = expression

Where:
> expression   is a valid Pascal expression.

Figure 3-30. The Pascal equal to operator.

Listing 3.21

```
{ list3-21.pas - Demonstrate the Pascal equal to operator }
program equal_to_operator;

begin
      writeln('1 = 1 is ', 1 = 1);
      writeln('2 = 1 is ', 2 = 1);
      writeln('1 = 2 is ', 1 = 2);
end.
```

LESSON 29. The Not Equal to Operator

The Pascal not equal to operator (<>) compares two expressions to see if they are unequal in value. If the two expressions are unequal, the not equal to operator returns a value of **True**. If the two expressions are equal, the not equal to operator returns a value of **False**. Figure 2.31 defines the not equal to operator.

The following examples illustrate the proper use of the not equal to operator:

> **Flag <> True**
> **count <> 2**
> **MouseButton <> Clicked**

Listing 3.22 demonstrates how the Pascal not equal to operator is used in an actual program.

---

expression <> expression

Where:
      expression   is a valid Pascal expression.

Figure 3-31. The Pascal not equal to operator.

Listing 3.22

```
{ list3-22.pas - Demonstrate the Pascal not equal to
operator }
program not_equal_to_operator;

begin
    writeln('1 <> 1 is ', 1 <> 1);
    writeln('2 <> 1 is ', 2 <> 1);
    writeln('1 <> 2 is ', 1 <> 2);
end.
```

LESSON 30. The Greater Than Operator

The Pascal greater than operator (>) compares two expressions to see if the first expression is greater than the second expression. If the first expression is greater than the second expression, the greater than operator returns a value of **True**. If the first expression in less than or equal to the second expression, the greater than operator returns a value of **False**. Figure 3-32 defines the greater than operator.

The following examples illustrate the proper use of the greater than operator:

n > 1
count > maximum
mouse_column > 80

Listing 3.23 demonstrates how the Pascal greater than operator is used in an actual program.

expression > expression

Where:
      expression   is a valid Pascal expression.

Figure 3-32. The Pascal greater than operator.

Listing 3.23

```
{ list3-23.pas - Demonstrate the Pascal greater than
operator }
program greater_than_operator;

begin
     writeln('1 > 1 is ', 1 > 1);
     writeln('2 > 1 is ', 2 > 1);
     writeln('1 > 2 is ', 1 > 2);
end.
```

LESSON 31. The Greater Than or Equal to Operator

The Pascal greater than or equal to operator (>=) compares two expressions to see if the first expression is greater than or equal to the second expression. If the first expression is greater than or equal to the second expression, the greater than or equal to operator returns a value of **True**. If the first expression is less than the second expression, the greater than or equal to operator returns a value of **False**. Figure 3-33 defines the greater than or equal to operator.

The following examples illustrate the proper use of the greater than or equal to operator:

> **count >= 55**
> **DisplayRow >= 23**
> **n >= 5**

Listing 3.24 demonstrates how the Pascal greater than or equal to operator is used in an actual program.

---

expression >= expression

Where:
      expression   is a valid Pascal expression.

Figure 3-33. The Pascal greater than or equal to operator.

Listing 3.24

```
{ list3-24.pas - Demonstrate the Pascal greater than or
equal to operator }
program greater_than_or_equal_to_operator;

begin
    writeln('1 >= 1 is ', 1 >= 1);
    writeln('2 >= 1 is ', 2 >= 1);
    writeln('1 >= 2 is ', 1 >= 2);
end.
```

LESSON 32.   The Less Than Operator

The Pascal less than operator (<) compares two expressions to see if the first expression is less than the second expression. If the first expression is less than the second expression, the less than operator returns a value of **True**. If the first expression is greater than or equal to the second expression, the less than operator returns a value of **False**. Figure 3-34 defines the less than operator.

The following examples illustrate the proper use of the less than operator:

> **n < 3**
> **MouseRow < 0**
> **counter < 55**

Listing 3.25 demonstrates how the Pascal less than operator is used in an actual program.

---

expression < expression

Where:

expression   is a valid Pascal expression.

Figure 3-34. The Pascal less than operator.

Listing 3.25

```
{ list3-25.pas - Demonstrate the Pascal less than operator }
program less_than_operator;

begin
     writeln('1 < 1 is ', 1 < 1);
     writeln('2 < 1 is ', 2 < 1);
     writeln('1 < 2 is ', 1 < 2);
end.
```

LESSON 33. The Less Than or Equal to Operator

The Pascal less than or equal to operator (<=) compares two expressions to see if the first expression is less than or equal to the second expression. If the first expression is less than or equal to the second expression, the less than or equal to operator returns a value of **True**. If the first expression in greater than the second expression, the less than or equal to operator returns a value of **False**. Figure 3-35 defines the less than or equal to operator.

The following examples illustrate the proper use of the less than or equal to operator:

> **count <= 5**
> **DisplayColumn <= 78**
> **n <= 3**

Listing 3.26 demonstrates how the Pascal less than or equal to operator is used in an actual program.

---

expression <= expression

Where:
      expression   is a valid Pascal expression.

Figure 3-35. The Pascal less than or equal to operator.

Listing 3.26

```
{ list3-26.pas - Demonstrate the Pascal less than or equal
to operator }
program less_than_or_equal_to_operator;

begin
     writeln('1 <= 1 is ', 1 <= 1);
     writeln('2 <= 1 is ', 2 <= 1);
     writeln('1 <= 2 is ', 1 <= 2);
end.
```

LESSON 34. Operator Precedence

Evaluating an expression with only one operator type is fairly straightforward. For example, the expression **2 + 3 + 6** is evaluated in two separate steps: 1) the expression **2 + 3** is figured and a result of **5** is returned and 2) the **6** is added to the previous result. Accordingly, the expression returns a value of **11**.

When expressions have the same operator type, Pascal simply evaluates them from left to right. But how does Pascal evaluate expressions that have more than one operator type? How, for example, does it evaluate the expression **2 + 3 * 6**?

If Pascal was to evaluate the **2 + 3** portion of the expression first, the result would be determined as follows:

    2 + 3 * 6
      5 * 6 = 30

But if Pascal was to evaluate the **3 * 6** portion of the expression first, the result would be determined as follows:

    2 + 3 * 6 = ?
    2 + 18 = 20

It's rather obvious that the two different methods for evaluating the expression return vastly different results. The Pascal programming language uses a set of rules called operator precedence to evaluate expressions in order to overcome these types of conflicts. Essentially, Pascal assigns a precedence level for each of its operators. When an expression is evaluated, the subexpression (one of the individual expressions that make up a more complex expression) that contains the operators with the highest precedence is evaluated first, the subexpression that contains the operators with the next highest precedence is evaluated second, and so on. This method continues until the portion of the expression with the lowest precedence has been evaluated.

Figure 3-36 defines the precedence levels that Pascal assigns to its wide range of operators. (Note that two of these operators—**@** and **in**—haven't been covered yet. These operators are used with some of Pascal's more advanced data types and will be discussed in Chapter 6.)

As figure 3-36 shows, some of the operators have equal levels of precedence. Whenever Pascal encounters two or more subexpressions with operators of equal precedence, they are evaluated on a strictly left-to-right basis.

It is possible to override the Pascal precedence rules by simply surrounding a subexpression with parentheses. Surrounding a subexpression with parentheses tells Pascal to evaluate the subexpression first.

For example, the expression **5 * 3 - 2** would be evaluated as follows:

```
5 * 3 - 2 = ?
  15  - 2 = 13
```

On the other hand, the expression **5 * (3 - 2)** would be evaluated as follows:

```
5 * (3 - 2) = ?
5 *   1   = 5
```

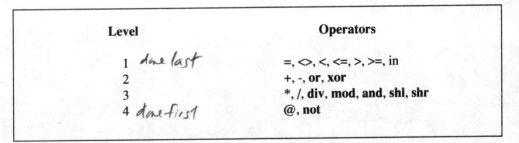

Level	Operators
1 *done last*	=, <>, <, <=, >, >=, in
2	+, -, **or**, **xor**
3	*, /, **div**, **mod**, **and**, **shl**, **shr**
4 *done first*	**@**, **not**

Figure 3-36. The Pascal operator precedence levels.

What if you had an expression, such as **150 div ((4 - 2) * 3)**, with nested (one inside the other) parentheses? Pascal would interpret such an expression by evaluating the the innermost subexpression first. Thus, the expression **150 div ((4 - 2) * 3)** would be evaluated as follows:

> **150 div ((4 - 2) * 3) = ?**
> **150 div (2 * 3) = ?**
> **150 div 6 = 25**

Listing 3.27 demonstrates how Pascal evaluates a variety of expressions.

Listing 3.27

```
{ list3.27.pas - Demonstrate Pascal precedence rules }
program precedence;

begin
     writeln('1 + 3 * 4 = ?');
     writeln('1 +    ', 3 * 4, ' = ', 1 + 3 * 4);
     writeln('150 div ((4 - 2) * 3) = ?');
     writeln('150 div (   ', 4 - 2, '    * 3) = ?');
     writeln('150 div           ', 2 * 3, ' = ', 150
div ((4 - 2) * 3));
end.
```

***

You now know how to use the Pascal operators to manipulate data. You are also familiar with the principle of operator precedence. Chapter 4 describes Pascal's program flow.

Chapter 4

Program Flow

This chapter describes Pascal's program flow, which can be summarized as follows. Pascal begins executing at the program's main body **begin** statement. Except for when it calls a procedure or function or encounters a program flow keyword, the program executes from the top of the main body to the bottom, until it reaches the main body's **end** statement. In addition to examining this basic structure, this chapter introduces you to the program flow keywords and shows you how they are used in actual programs. It also discusses **while**, **repeat,** and **for** loops, as well as **if**, **case**, and **goto** statements.

LESSON 35. While Loops

The Pascal **while** keyword tells the program to continuously execute a statement until a condition is no longer true. Figure 4-1 defines the **while** keyword and shows how it is used in a **while** loop. The statement to be executed can be either a single program statement or a multi-statement **begin..end** block.

```
        while condition do
                statement;
            or
        while condition do
        begin
                statement;
                .
                .
                statement;
        end;

        Where:
                condition              is a valid boolean expression.

                statement              is a valid program statement.
```

Figure 4-1. The while keyword.

Listing 4.1 demonstrates how the Pascal **while** keyword is used in a program that displays every odd number between 100 and 200.

Listing 4.1

```
{ list4-1.pas - Demonstrate the Pascal while keyword }
program while_loop1;

var
      number : integer;

begin
      number := 101;
      while number < 201 do
      begin
              writeln('number = ', number);
  continued...
```

...from previous page
```
            number := number + 2;
      end;
end.
```

To better understand how the while keyword works, take a closer look at Listing 4.1's main program body.

number := 101;
assigns the value 101 to the **integer** variable **number**.

while number < 201 do
checks the value of **number**. If **number** is less than 201, the **while** statement is executed. If **number** is greater than or equal to 201, the **while** statement is ignored.

writeln('number = ', number);
displays **number's** current value.

number := number + 2;
increases the value of **number** to the next odd value. After executing this statement, the program loops back to the **while** keyword.

You may be wondering what happens if the **while** condition is initially **False**. The while statement would never be executed. For example, the following while loop would never be executed:

while False do
  i = i + 1

The initial condition is **False**. Consequently, the statement **i = i + 1** will never be executed.

LESSON 36. Repeat Loops

The Pascal **repeat** keyword is similar to the **while** keyword. The only difference between the two is that the **repeat** keyword checks for a condition after it executes its associated program statement. Therefore, a **repeat** loop is, in a sense, a backwards **while** loop. Figure 4-2 defines the **repeat** keyword and its use in constructing a **repeat** loop. The **repeat** statement can be either a single program statement or a multi-statement **begin..end** block.

```
        repeat
                statement
        until condition;
        or
        repeat
        begin
                statement;
                .
                .
                statement;
        end;
        until condition

        Where:
                condition                      is a valid boolean expression.

                statement                      is a valid program statement.
```

Figure 4-2. The repeat keyword.

Listing 4.2 demonstrates how the Pascal repeat keyword is used in a program that displays every odd number between 100 and 200.

Listing 4.2

```
{ list4-2.pas - Demonstrate the Pascal repeat keyword }
program repeat_loop;

var
      number : integer;

begin
      number := 101;
      repeat
      begin
              writeln('number = ', number);
              number := number + 2;
      end;
      until number > 199;
end.
```

To better understand how the repeat keyword works, take a closer look at Listing 4.2's main program body.

> *number := 101;*
> assigns the value 101 to the **integer** variable **number**.

> *repeat*
> causes the next statement to be executed.

> *writeln('number = ', number);*
> displays **number's** current value.

> *number := number + 2;*
> increases the value of **number** to the next odd value.

> *until number > 199;*
> checks to see if the last odd value has been displayed. If the last odd value hasn't been displayed, program execution loops back to the **repeat** keyword.

Note that a **repeat** loop is always executed at least once. As in the above example, the **repeat** statement is executed before the condition is checked. Therefore, the statement is always executed at least once.

LESSON 37. For Loops

The Pascal **for** keyword is used to tell the program to execute a statement for a set number of times. Figure 4-3 defines the **for** keyword and its use in constructing a **for** loop.

As Figure 4-3 illustrates, the **for** statement assigns the value of an expression to a variable. Note that the expressions in a **for** statement must return an ordinal result. Ordinal numbers are covered in detail in Chapter 6, but for now think of them as any integer.

If the **to** keyword is used in the **for** statement, program execution continues by checking to see if the variable's value is less than or equal to the value of the **for** statement's second expression. If the variable's value is less than or equal to the value of the second expression, the statement after the **do** keyword is executed. After the **do** statement is executed, the variable is incremented (variable := variable + 1) and its contents are once again checked against the result of the second expression.

```
for identifier := expression to expression do
        statement;
    or
for identifier := expression to expression do
begin
        statement;
        .
        .
        statement;
end;
    or
for identifier := expression downto expression do
        statement;
    or
for identifier := expression downto expression do
begin
        statement;
        .
        .
        statement;
end;


Where:
        identifier              is a valid variable or typed constant
                                identifier.

        expression              is a valid Pascal expression.

        statement               is a valid program statement.
```

Figure 4-3. The for keyword.

If the **downto** keyword is used in the **for** statement, program execution continues after variable initialization by checking to see if the variable's value is greater than or equal to the value of the **for** statement's second expression. If the variable's value is greater than or equal to the value of the second expression, the statement following the **do** keyword is executed next. After the **do** statement is executed, the variable is decremented (variable := variable - 1) and its contents are once again checked against the result of the second expression.

Listing 4.3 demonstrates how the Pascal for keyword is used in a program that displays every number between 60 and 100 in ascending order.

Listing 4.3

```
{ list4-3.pas - Demonstrate an ascending for loop }
program ascending_for;

var
     cnt : integer;

begin
     for cnt := 60 to 100 do
          writeln('cnt = ', cnt);
end.
```

Listing 4.4 demonstrates a descending **for** loop by displaying every number between 60 and 100 in descending order.

Listing 4.4

```
{ list4-4.pas - Demonstrate a descending for loop }
program descending_for;

var
     cnt : integer;
```
continued...

...from previous page
```
begin
     for cnt := 100 downto 60 do
           writeln('cnt = ', cnt);
end.
```

Note that whenever the **for** variable's initial value exceeds the value of the second expression in a **for..to..do** combination or is smaller than the value of the second expression in a **for..downto..do** combination, the statement following the **do** will never be executed. For example, neither the statement **for i := 1 to 0 do** or the statement **for i := 0 downto 1 do** would ever cause its associated **do** statements to be executed.

LESSON 38. If Statements

Many times a program will have to do different things depending on a certain condition. To meet these conditional demands, Pascal is equipped with a variety of decision-making statements. The simplest Pascal decision-making statement is the **if..then** statement. Figure 4-4 defines the construction of an **if..then** statement.

```
     if expression then
           statement;
        or
     if expression then
     begin
           statement;
           .
           .
           statement;
     end;

Where:
           expresssion              is a valid boolean expression.

           statement                is a valid Pascal statement.
```

Figure 4-4. The Pascal if..then statement.

The logic behind a Pascal **if..then** statement is simple. **If** the boolean expression following the **if** keyword is equal to **True**, **then** the program statement following the **then** keyword is executed.

Listing 4.5 demonstrates how an **if** statement is used in an actual Pascal program.

Listing 4.5

```
{ list4-5.pas - Demonstrate the Pascal if..then statement }
program if_then_demo;

var
      number : integer;

begin
      number := 1;
      if number = 1 then
            writeln('number is equal to 1');
      if number = 0 then
            writeln('number is equal to 0');
end.
```

In addition to being able to perform an action if a condition is **True**, an **if** statement can also perform another action if a condition is **False** by using an **else** clause. Figure 4-5 defines the construction of an **if..then..else** statement.

The logic behind an **if..then..else** statement is easy to understand. **If** the condition is **True**, **then** the program statement following the **then** keyword is executed, **else** the statement following the **else** keyword is executed.

Listing 4.6 demonstrates how an **if..then..else** statement is used in an actual Pascal program.

Listing 4.6

```
{ list4-6.pas - Demonstrate the Pascal if..then..else statement }
program if_then_else;
```
continued...

...from previous page

```
var
        number : integer;

begin
        number := 1;
        if number = 1 then
                writeln('number is equal to 1')
        else
                writeln('number isn''t equal to 1');
        number := 0;
        if number = 1 then
                writeln('number is equal to 1')
        else
                writeln('number isn''t equal to 1');
end.
```

---

if expression **then**
      statement;
else
      statement;
     or
if expression **then**
begin
      statement;
      .
      .
      statement;
end
else
begin
      statement;
      .
      .
      statement;
end;

Where:
      expression   is a valid boolean expression.

Figure 4-5. The Pascal if..then..else statement.

LESSON 39. Case Statements

Although **if..then** and **if..then..else** statements are useful for performing actions depending on a condition being either **True** or **False**, many situations arise in a program that require a variety of actions to be performed depending on an ordinal expression's value. To meet this requirement, Pascal provides the **case** statement.

The case constants in a Pascal **case** statement can be either a single constant, a group of constants, or a range of constants. If the value of the **case** statement's expression matches any of a constant group's individual constants, the group's associated program statement is executed. The following are some examples of constant groups:

100, 101, 102
-55, 32, 8
36, 1

Figure 4-6 defines the construction of a **case** statement.

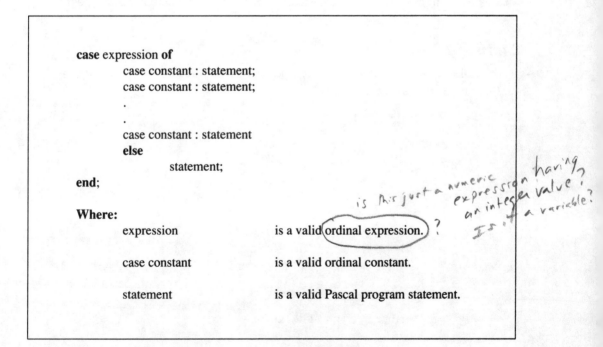

```
case expression of
      case constant : statement;
      case constant : statement;
      .
      .
      case constant : statement
      else
            statement;
end;

Where:
      expression              is a valid ordinal expression.

      case constant           is a valid ordinal constant.

      statement               is a valid Pascal program statement.
```

is this just a numeric expression having an integer value? Is it a variable?

Figure 4-6. The Pascal case statement.

If the value of the **case** statement's expression falls anywhere within a range of constants, the range's associated program statement is executed. The following are some examples of constant ranges:

100..300
-5..5
2000...100000

Figure 4-6 also shows that Pascal supports **else** clauses in a **case** statement. As with the **if..then** statement, **else** clauses in a **case** statement are strictly optional. If used, their associated program statement is only executed if the **case** statement's expression doesn't match any of the case constants. If an **else** clause isn't used and the **case** statement's expression doesn't match any of the case constants, the whole **case** statement is ignored and program execution continues with the next program statement.

Listing 4.7 demonstrates how a **case** statement is used in an actual Pascal program.

Listing 4.7

```
{ list4-7.pas - Demonstrate the Pascal case statement }
program case_statement;

var
      number : Integer;

begin
      number := 3;
      case number of
            1 : writeln('The number is a 1');
            2 : writeln('The number is a 2');
            3..5 : writeln('The number is a 3, 4, or 5');
            7, 10 : writeln('The number is a 7 or 10');
            8 : writeln('The number is an 8');
            9 : writeln('The number is a 9');
            else
                  writeln('The number isn''t between 1 and 10');
      end;
end.
```

LESSON 40. Goto Statements

Sometimes program execution must branch to a different part of a program without regard for any condition. Pascal provides the **goto** statement for performing such an unconditional jump. You should be aware, however, that today the use of the **goto** statement is considered poor programming practice. Although the **goto** statement is necessary for some other languages (i.e., BASIC), you can go through your whole life without finding it necessary to use a **goto** statement in a Pascal program. Perhaps its only acceptable use today is in implementing critical error handling routines. Always strive to write your programs without using **gotos**. *Yes Sir!*

Figure 4-7 defines the construction of a Pascal **goto** statement. Note that the **goto** statement requires a label to direct it where to branch. A Pascal label can be any series of digits in the range of 0 to 9999, or it can be an identifier.

---

goto label;

Where:
         label   is a valid Pascal label.

Figure 4-7. The Pascal goto statement.

Listing 4.8 demonstrates how a goto statement is used in an actual program.

Listing 4.8

```
{ list4-8.pas - Demonstrate the Pascal goto statement }
program goto_demo;

label 1;        is this needed ?

begin
     writeln('This line is executed');
     goto 1;
     writeln('This line never is!');
1:
     writeln('This line is executed too');
end.
```

***

You're now familiar with Pascal's flow keywords and know how to use **while**, **repeat**, and **for** loops, as well as **if, case**, and **goto** statements in actual programs. Chapter 5 introduces you to procedures and functions.

Chapter 5

Procedures and Functions

In most programs you write, you find that certain routines are used repeatedly. Listing 5.1, for example, demonstrates how an **if..then..else** statement is used over and over to conditionally display messages. This chapter introduces you to procedures and functions—Pascal's "programs within programs" that allow you to avoid rewriting frequently-used routines. The chapter teaches you how to declare procedures and functions. It also explains function return values, forward declarations, local variables, scope, arguments, nested procedures/functions, and recursion.

Listing 5.1

```
{ list5-1.pas - Display messages program }
program display_messages;
   continued...
```

...from previous page

```
var
      number : integer;

begin
      number := 1;
      if number = 1 then
            writeln('number is equal to 1')
      else
            writeln('number isn''t equal to 1');
      number := 0;
      if number = 1 then
            writeln('number is equal to 1')
      else
            writeln('number isn''t equal to 1');
end.
```

LESSON 41. Declaring Procedures and Functions

Pascal's functions and procedures eliminate the necessity of repeatedly writing the same conditional statement. Not only can it have its own body of program statements, a procedure or a function can have its own variables, typed constants, and procedures and functions. Figure 5-1 defines the format for defining a prodecure. Figure 5-2 defines the format for declaring a function.

Like the program's main body, a procedure's or a function's associated program statements are enclosed in a **begin..end** statement block. Figures 5-1 and 5-2 show that procedures and functions can also have an optional parameter list. A procedure's or function's parameters are used to pass values to the procedure or function. The following are some examples of parameter lists:

(row, col : integer; message : string)
(x, y : integer)
(name : string)

Note in the above examples that the parameters are defined as they would be in a variable definition. Also note how each data type is separated by a semicolon, just as a normal program statement. However, the final parameter declaration in a parameter list doesn't require a semicolon.

```
procedure name(parameter list);
begin
        statement;
        .
        .
        statement;
end;

Where:
        name                            is the procedure's identifier.

        parameter list                  is a list of arguments to be passed to the
                                        procedure.

        statement                       is a valid Pascal program statement.
```

Figure 5-1. A Pascal procedure declaration.

```
function name(parameter list)  :  return type;
begin
        statement;
        .
        .
        statement;
end;

Where:
        name                            is the function's identifier.

        parameter list                  is a list of arguments to be passed to the
                                        procedure.

        return type                     is a previously defined data type.

        statement                       is a valid Pascal program statement.
```

Figure 5-2. A Pascal function definition.

Listing 5.2 demonstrates how a procedure is used in an actual Pascal program. Unlike the program in Listing 5.1, this newer version uses a procedure to replace the multiple **if..then..else** statements.

Listing 5.2

```
{ list5-2.pas - Display messages program version 2}
program display_messages2;

procedure display(n : integer);
begin
      if n = 1 then
            writeln('The number is equal to 1')
      else
            writeln('The number isn''t equal to 1');
end;

var
      number : integer;

begin
      number := 1;
      display(number);
      number := 0;
      display(number);
end.
```

Although Listing 5.2 is a simple example of how a procedure is used in Pascal, it demonstrates important points about using a procedure or a function in a program. It's helpful to take a line by-line look at both the **display** procedure and the program's main body.

> *procedure display(n : integer);*
> defines a procedure named **display** that has one integer argument identified by **n**.

> *begin*
> defines the start of **display's** statement block.

if n = 1 then
> *writeln('The number is equal to 1')*
else
> *writeln('The number isn''t equal to 1');*

displays the message **The number is equal to 1** if argument **n** is equal to **1**. Otherwise, it displays the message **The number isn't equal to 1**.

end;

defines the end of **display's** statement block.

begin

defines the start of the program's main body.

number := 1;

assigns the value **1** to the **integer** variable **number**.

display(number);

calls the procedure **display**. Additionally, the value of the **integer** variable **number** is passed as **display's** one and only argument.

number := 0;

assigns the value **0** to the **integer** variable **number**.

display(number);

calls the procedure **display**. Additionally, the value of the **integer** variable **number** is passed as **display's** one and only argument.

end.

defines the end of the program's main body.

LESSON 42. Function Return Values

Now that you've seen how a simple procedure is written, take a look at how a simple function is written. A function declaration requires that you specify a return type. For example, you must declare a function that returns an **integer** value as returning an **integer** data type.

Although declaring the function's return type is fairly simple, it is not so obvious how the function's return value is actually returned to the calling program. Fortunately for the Pascal programmer, a value is returned by simply assigning the function's return value to the function's identifier. The function's identifier acts like a variable with the data type defined as the function's return type. For example, a function named **intadd** returns a value of 2 to the calling program as follows:

> intadd := 2;

This example shows that returning a value to the calling program requires nothing more than a simple assignment statement. Listing 5.3 calls a simple function that multiplies a passed argument by 2 and returns the result.

Listing 5.3

```
{ list5-3.pas - Demonstrates Pascal functions }
program function_calls;

function times_two(n : integer) : integer;
begin
      times_two := n * 2;
end;

begin
      writeln(times_two(4));
      writeln(times_two(16));
end.
```

In order to fully understand how the above program performs its task, its helpful to examine the **times_two** function and the program's main body a line at a time.

> *function times_two(n : integer) : integer;*
> defines a function named **times_two** that has one **integer** argument identified by **n** and returns an **integer** value.

> *begin*
> defines the start of **times_two's** statement block.

> *times_two := n * 2;*
> multiplies argument **n** by **2** and assigns it to the function's identifier **times_two**.

> *end;*
> defines the end of the **times_two** statement block.

begin
defines the start of the program's main body.

writeln(times_two(4));
displays the result of multiplying 4 times 2.

writeln(times_two(16));
displays the result of multiplying 16 times 2.

end.
defines the end of the program's main body.

LESSON 43. Forward Declarations

Suppose that you want to write a program with a procedure that calls another procedure. This is a common occurrence in Pascal. Is there a special way you have to write such a program? As a matter of fact, there is. You can write your program using either one of two methods: the easiest method is demonstrated in Listing 5.4.

Listing 5.4

```
{ list5-4.pas - Demonstrate procedure calling procedures }
program procedure_calling;

procedure first;
begin
     writeln('This is the first procedure.');
end;

procedure second;
begin
     first;
     writeln('This is the second procedure.');
end;

begin
     second;
end.
```

Pascal requires that a procedure that will be called by another procedure be defined before the procedure that calls it. What would happen if the called procedure wasn't defined first? The simplest way to find out is to enter the program in Listing 5.5 and compile it.

Listing 5.5

```
{ list5-5.pas - Demonstrate an incorrect declaration }
program incorrect_declaration;

procedure second;
begin
     first;
     writeln('This is the second procedure.');
end;

procedure first;
begin
     writeln('This is the first procedure.');
end;

begin
     second;
end.
```

With the exception of defining procedure **second** before procedure **first**, Listing 5.5 is the same as Listing 5.4. If you took the time to enter and compile Listing 5.5, you would be informed that the **first** identifier in procedure **second** is an unknown identifier. Why is **first** an unknown identifier? It has no meaning in the program yet. Unless you define procedure **first** before procedure **second**, the Pascal compiler has no way of knowing what the identifier **first** represents. As far as the compiler is concerned, **first** could be a variable, a constant, or anything else for which a Pascal identifier is used. The compiler has to abort the compilation process and return the rather disappointing error message.

Fortunately for the Pascal programmer, there is a way around having to define a called procedure or function before the calling procedure or function. The method used to perform this trick is called a **forward declaration**. Figure 5-3 defines the structure of a forward declaration. You make a forward declaration by following a procedure or function head with the keyword **forward**. Once you do this, any other procedure or function will be able to call the forward declaration's associated procedure or function.

---

procedure name(parameter list) **; forward;**
    or
function name(parameter list) **:** return type; **forward;**

Where:

name	is the procedure's or function's identifier.
return type	is a previously defined data type.
parameter list	is a list of arguments to be passed by the procedure or function.

Figure 5-3. A forward declaration.

Listing 5.6 demonstrates how Listing 5.5 could be correctly rewritten by adding a forward declaration before procedure **second**.

Listing 5.6

```
{ list5-6.pas - Demonstrate a forward declaration }
program forward_declaration;

procedure first; forward;

procedure second;
begin
     first;
     writeln('This is the second procedure.');
end;

procedure first;
```
continued...

...from previous page
```
begin
      writeln('This is the first procedure.');
end;

begin
      second;
end.
```

LESSON 44. Local Variables

As stated earlier in this chapter, a Pascal procedure or function can have its own variables, called local variables. Local variables can be used only inside of the procedure or function. The reason for this is scope, a concept that is discussed in the next lesson. Figure 5-4 defines the format of the variables in a procedure or function.

```
            procedure or function head;
      var
                  variable declaration;
                  .
                  .
                  variable declaration;

      begin
                  statement;
                  .
                  .
                  statement;
      end;

      Where:
                  procedure or function head   is a valid procedure or function head.

                  variable declaration         is a valid variable declaration.

                  statement                    is a valid program statement.
```

Figure 5-4. Procedure and function variables.

The variable declarations are placed in between the procedure's or function's head and its associated body. You can declare typed constants in a procedure or a function by using this same method. Listing 5.7 demonstrates how local variables are used in an actual Pascal program that uses the local variable **i** to count from 1 to 10 each time the procedure **count** is called.

Listing 5.7

```
{ list5-7.pas - Demonstrate local variables }
program local_variables;

procedure count;
var
     i : integer;
begin
     i := 1;
     while i < 11 do
     begin
          writeln(i);
          i := i + 1;
     end;
end;

begin
     count;
     count;
end.
```

Listing 5.8 demonstrates how typed constants are used in an actual Pascal program.

Listing 5.8

```
{ list5-8.pas - Demonstrate local typed constants }
program local_typed_constants;

procedure count;
const
     i : integer = 1;
```
continued...

...from previous page

```
begin
      writeln(i);
      i := i + 1;
end;

begin
      count;
      count;
end.
```

Listing 5.8 demonstrates an interesting fact about typed constants. Remember that typed constants retain their value until the program finishes executing. Thus, the first time the procedure **count** is called it displays a value of **1** for the typed constant **i**. The second time it is called, **count** displays a value of **2**, the third time it is called it displays a value of **3**, and so on.

Although Listing 5.8 demonstrates how a typed constant retains its value between procedure and function calls, you may wonder what happens with a procedure's or a function's variables between function calls. Do they still retain their values like a typed constant? No. Like a variable in the main program, a local variable is undefined at the start of the procedure or function call.

Listing 5.9 demonstrates how a local variable is in an undefined state at the start of procedure call. With the single exception of declaring **i** as a variable instead of a typed constant, Listing 5.9 is the same as Listing 5.8. However, this simple change reflects how a local variable is considered undefined each time a procedure or a function is called.

Listing 5.9

```
{ list5-9.pas - Demonstrate how variables are undefined }
program undefined;

procedure count;
var
      i : integer;

begin
    continued...
```

...from previous page
```
        writeln(i);
        i := i + 1;
end;

begin
        count;
        count;
end.
```

LESSON 45. Scope

Lesson 44 explained that procedure and function variables are called local variables because of something called scope. This lesson examines how a variable's scope affects what parts of a program can access it. Procedure and function variables are called local variables (only the variable's procedure or function can access them). Thus, all procedure and function variables are said to have local scope.

What about the variables that are defined outside a procedure or function? They are called global variables. Global variables can be accessed by any procedure, function, or part of the program's main body that follows its declaration. Listing 5.10 demonstrates how a variable with global scope can be accessed by a procedure.

Listing 5.10
```
{ list5-10.pas - Demonstrate global scope }
program global_scope;

var
        i : integer;

procedure display_i;
begin
        writeln(i);
        i := i + 1;
end;

begin
```
continued...

91

...from previous page
```
      i := 1;
      display_i;
      writeln(i);
end.
```

Not only does Listing 5.10's procedure **display_i** display global variable **i's** value, it increments **i** before returning to the program's main body. After execution is returned to the program's main body, **i's** new value is displayed.

What if a procedure or a function had a local variable named **i** in addition to a global variable **i**? This situation is fairly common in most programs. How does a procedure or function know which **i** to choose? The procedure or function will always use its local variable **i**. This concept is demonstrated in Listing 5.11.

Listing 5.11

```
{ list5-11.pas - Demonstrate global vs. local scope }
program global_vs_local_scope;

var
      i : integer;

procedure display_i;
var
      i : integer;

begin
      i := 999;
      writeln(i);
      i := i + 1;
end;

begin
      i := 1;
      display_i;
      writeln(i);
end.
```

Listing 5.11 illustrates that the procedure **display_i** has no effect on the global variable **i**. The procedure **display_i** displays its own local variable **i**, needlessly adds it, and returns to the program's main body. When execution is returned to the program's main body, the global variable **i** is displayed to show that it hasn't been changed.

LESSON 46. Arguments

The previous lessons have shown that arguments (or parameters) can be passed to either a procedure or a function. Usually, an argument is **passed by value** (the argument's value is passed to the function). This concept may seem obvious, but it is important. For example, Listing 5.12 passes global variable **n's** value to the procedure **count**. Once it is passed to the procedure, the argument's value is displayed and decremented over and over until it is less than zero. Note that upon return from procedure **count**, global variable **n's** value is displayed to prove that it hasn't been changed by the procedure.

Listing 5.12

```
{ list5-12.pas - Demonstrate passing by value }
program pass_by_value;

var
     n : integer;

procedure count(number : integer);
begin
     repeat
          writeln(number);
          number := number - 1;
     until number < 0;
end;

begin
     n := 10;
     count(n);
     writeln(n);
end.
```

Although passing by value is the most common method Pascal programmers use when passing arguments, Pascal offers another method for passing arguments: **passing by reference**. You pass arguments by reference by placing the **var** keyword before the argument declaration in the procedure or function head. The following examples illustrate argument declarations that are passed by reference:

> **var row, col : integer;**
> **var account : real;**

Passing an argument by reference actually passes the argument's memory location and not its value. With the argument's memory location at its disposal, the procedure or function is able to directly access and modify the passed argument. Because the procedure or function needs the argument's actual location in memory, an expression can't be passed by reference. Why would you want to modify the value of an expression that lies outside the procedure or function? Once its value has been passed to the procedure or function, the expression serves no useful purpose, thus you should remember to always pass expressions by value.

Listing 5.13 demonstrates how an argument is passed by reference. Unlike Listing 5.12, this modified version passes the procedure **count's** argument **number** by reference. This results in global variable **n's** value being modified by procedure **count**. Upon return from the procedure **count**, global variable **n** has a value of **-1** and not the value of **10** that it had in Listing 5.12.

Listing 5.13

```
{ list5-13.pas - Demonstrate passing by reference }
program pass_by_reference;

var
      n : integer;

procedure count(var number : integer);
begin
      repeat
            writeln(number);
            number := number - 1;
```

indicates passing arguments by reference

continued...

...from previous page
```
      until number < 0;
end;
begin
      n := 10;
      count(n);
      writeln(n);
end.
```

LESSON 47. Nested Procedures and Functions

In addition to being able to have its own variables, a Pascal procedure or function can also have its own procedures and functions (nested procedures and functions). The easiest way to imagine how a procedure or function can have its own procedures and functions is to think of a Pascal program as nothing more than an extra large procedure that contains other defineable procedures and functions. Figure 5-5 defines the structure of nested procedures and functions.

```
      procedure or function head;

              procedure or function head;
              begin
                      statement;
                      .
                      .
                      statement;
              end;

      begin
          statement;
          .
          .
          statement;
      end;

      Where:
              procedure or function head   is a valid procedure or function head.

              statement                    is a valid program statement.
```

Figure 5-5. Nested Pascal procedures and functions.

Listing 5.14 demonstrates how a function can be nested in a procedure.

Listing 5.14

```
{ list5-14.pas - Demonstrate nested procedures and functions }
program nested_p_and_f;

procedure display(n : integer);
var
      i : integer;
      function addone(n : integer) : integer;
      begin
            addone := n + 1;
      end;

begin
      for i := 1 to 10 do
      begin
            writeln(n);
            n := addone(n);
      end;
end;

begin
      display(1);
end.
```

a procedure

Listing 5.14 displays a number, adds one to it, and repeats the process nine more times. When studying this program, remember to use the analogy that a Pascal program is nothing more than a big procedure or, conversely, a procedure is nothing more than a miniature program. Keeping that in mind will help make writing individual nested procedures and functions easy.

To write your own nested procedures and functions correctly, you must understand how Pascal's scope rules apply to procedures and functions. Like a procedure's or a function's local variables, a nested procedure or function is local to the procedure or function in which it is defined. Listing 5.15 demonstrates how the Pascal scope rules work by defining two functions with the same name. Because of the scope rules, the function **addone** inside of the procedure **display** is called rather than the global function **addone**.

Listing 5.15

```
{ list5-15.pas - Demonstrate procedure and function }
program p_and_f_scope;

function addone(n : integer) : integer;
begin
      addone := n + 101;
end;

procedure display(n : integer);
var
      i : integer;
      function addone(n :  integer) : integer;
      begin
            addone := n + 1;
      end;

begin
      for i := 1 to 10 do
      begin
            writeln(n);
            n := addone(n);
      end;
end;

begin
      display(1);
end.
```

LESSON 48. Recursion

Pascal procedures and functions posess **recursion**. Recursion allows a Pascal procedure or function to call itself repeatedly. Although this may not seem to be an important feature, recursion can simplify writing some of the most important computer programming routines (i.e., quick sort, b-trees, etc.).

Listing 5.16 demonstrates how a Pascal procedure can recursively call itself.

Listing 5.16

```
{ list5-16.pas - Demonstrate recursion }
program recursion;

procedure count(n : integer);
begin
     writeln(n);
     n := n - 1;
     if n >= 0 then
          count(n);
end;

begin
     count(20);
end.
```

Although Listing 5.16 is simple, it's helpful to take a detailed look at how the procedure **count** is used to count backwards from a passed argument.

> *begin*
> defines the start of the procedure **count's** body.

> *writeln(n);*
> displays the **integer** argument **n's** value.

> *n := n - 1;*
> decrements **n's** value.

> *if n >= 0 then*
> > *count(n);*
> checks argument **n's** value to see if it is still greater than or equal to 0. If it is still greater than or equal to zero, **count** calls itself with **n's** new value for its argument.

> *end;*
> defines the end of the procedure **count's** body.

This routine could be simplified with a loop. However, there are a number of important computer programming routines that are much easier to write using recursion than with more traditional programming methods. Consequently, it is essential for Pascal programmers to understand how recursion works.

***

You now know how to declare procedures and functions and are familiar with the concepts of function return values, forward declarations, local variables, scope, arguments, nested procedures and functions, and recursion. Chapter 6 teaches you how to define your own data types.

Chapter 6

User-Defined Data Types

This chapter offers a new way of looking at program data: it illustrates how you can use various procedures, functions, and operators to define your own data types. The chapter also acquaints you with subranges and sets. The capacity to create user-defined data types is one of Pascal's main advantages over other programming languages.

LESSON 49. Enumerated Data Types

The type of user-defined data you will look at in this chapter is called enumerated data. You construct an enumerated data type from a list of unique identifiers. Each of the enumerated data type's identifiers are assigned a value of **0** to **n**, where **n** represents the number of identifiers minus one. For example, an enumerated data type with 10 identifiers would have assigned values of **0** to **9**. Figure 6-1 defines the structure of an enumerated data type.

```
        type
                data type identifier = (identifier list);

        Where:
                data type identifier        is a valid identifier.

                identifier list             is a list of valid identifiers. If more than one
                                            identifier is specified, they are separated by
                                            commas.
```

Figure 6-1. Defining a Pascal enumerated data type.

As figure 6-1 shows, an enumerated data type definition follows the **type** keyword. The following are some examples of enumerated data type declarations:

suit = (clubs, spades, hearts, diamonds);
computers = (IBM, Apple, Tandy, Commodore, Acer, Dell);

Listing 6.1 demonstrates how an enumerated data type is used in an actual Pascal program.

Listing 6.1

```
{ list6-1.pas - Demonstrate enumerated data types }
program enum_data;

type
        computers = (IBM, Apple, Tandy, Commodore, Other);

var
        Jim, David : computers;

procedure display_brand(brand : computers);
begin
        case brand of
                IBM:
```
continued...

...from previous page

```
                writeln(' has an IBM');
        Apple:
                writeln(' has an Apple');
        Tandy:
                writeln(' has a Tandy');
        Commodore:
                writeln(' has a Commodore');
        else
                writeln(' doesn''t have an IBM, Apple,
                Tandy, or Commodore');
        end
end;

begin
        Jim := IBM;
        David := Other;
        write('Jim');
        display_brand(Jim);
        write('David');
        display_brand(David);
end.
```

LESSON 50. The Dec Procedure

To allow programmers to easily handle enumerated data types or any other ordinal data types (those that are expressed as a series of whole numbers, integers, characters, etc.), Pascal comes equipped with a variety of ordinal-related procedures and functions. The first ordinal procedure you will study is the **dec** procedure. The Pascal **dec** procedure subtracts one from an ordinal variable's value. Figure 6-2 defines the structure of the Pascal **dec** procedure.

---

dec(ordinal variable);

Where:

        ordinal variable   is a valid Pascal ordinal variable.

Figure 6-2. The Pascal dec procedure.

Listing 6.2 demonstrates how the Pascal **dec** procedure is used in an actual program.

Listing 6.2

```
{ list6-2.pas - Demonstrate the Pascal dec function }
program dec_demo;

type
     cards = (clubs, diamonds, spades, hearts);

procedure display_suit(card : cards);
begin
     case card of
          clubs:
               writeln('The card is a club');
          diamonds:
               writeln('The card is a diamond');
          spades:
               writeln('The card is a spade');
          hearts:
               writeln('The card is a heart');
     end;
end;

var
     c1 : cards;

begin
     c1 := hearts;
     display_suit(c1);
     dec(c1);
     display_suit(c1);
end.
```

LESSON 51. The Inc Procedure

In Lesson 50 you learned that the Pascal **dec** procedure subtracts one from an ordinal variable's value. Conversely, the Pascal **inc** procedure adds one to an ordinal variable's value. Figure 6-3 defines the structure of the Pascal **inc** procedure.

```
    inc(ordinal variable);

    Where:
            ordinal variable          is a valid Pascal ordinal variable.
```

Figure 6-3. The Pascal inc procedure.

Listing 6.3 demonstrates how the Pascal **inc** procedure is used in an actual program.

Listing 6.3

```
{ list6-3.pas - Demonstrate the Pascal inc function }
program inc_demo;

type
      cards = (clubs, diamonds, spades, hearts);

procedure display_suit(card : cards);
begin
      case card of
            clubs:
                  writeln('The card is a club');
            diamonds:
                  writeln('The card is a diamond');
            spades:
                  writeln('The card is a spade');
            hearts:
                  writeln('The card is a heart');
      end;
end;

var
      c1 : cards;

begin
      c1 := clubs;
      display_suit(c1);
      inc(c1);
      display_suit(c1);
end.
```

LESSON 52. The Pred Function

The Pascal **pred** function returns the value of an ordinal expression minus one. Figure 6-4 defines the structure of the Pascal **pred** function.

---

pred(ordinal expression);

Where:

ordinal expression   is a valid Pascal ordinal expression.

Figure 6-4. The Pascal pred function.

Listing 6.4 demonstrates how the **pred** function is used in an actual Pascal program.

Listing 6.4

```
{ list6-4.pas - Demonstrate the Pascal pred function }
program pred_demo;

type
      cards = (clubs, diamonds, spades, hearts);

procedure display_suit(card : cards);
begin
      case card of
            clubs:
                  writeln('The card is a club');
            diamonds:
                  writeln('The card is a diamond');
            spades:
                  writeln('The card is a spade');
            hearts:
                  writeln('The card is a heart');
      end;
end;

var
      c1 : cards;
```
continued...

...from previous page
```
begin
     c1 := hearts;
     display_suit(c1);
     display_suit(pred(c1));
end.
```

this is an ordinal expression?

LESSON 53. The Succ Function

Pascal offers a compliment to the **pred** function called the **succ** function. The Pascal **succ** function returns the value of an ordinal expression plus one. Figure 6-5 defines the Pascal **succ** function.

---

succ(ordinal expression);

Where:
>   ordinal expression   is a valid Pascal ordinal expression.

Figure 6-5. The Pascal succ function.

Listing 6.5 demonstrates how the **succ** function is used in an actual Pascal program.

Listing 6.5

```
{ list6-5.pas - Demonstrate the Pascal succ function }
program succ_demo;

type
     cards = (clubs, diamonds, spades, hearts);

procedure display_suit(card : cards);
begin
     case card of
          clubs:
                writeln('The card is a club');
          diamonds:
                writeln('The card is a diamond');
          spades:
                writeln('The card is a spade');
```
continued...

...from previous page

```
          hearts:
                writeln('The card is a heart');
      end;
end;

var
      c1 : cards;

begin
      c1 := clubs;
      display_suit(c1);
      display_suit(succ(c1));
end.
```

LESSON 54. Subranges

Often you will want to limit a data type's range of values. For example, a data value representing the months of a year would only need values in the range of 1 to 12. Fortunately you can define new data types by using a subrange of another previously defined ordinal data type. Thus you can construct subrange data types from integers, characters, or enumerations.

Figure 6-6 defines a subrange data type.

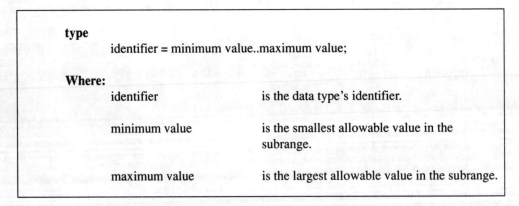

Figure 6-6. Defining a subrange data type.

The following examples illustrate valid integer and character subrange data type definitions:

rows = 1..25;
columns = 1..80;
dice = 1..6;
month = 1..12;
day = 1..31;
numeric = '0'..'9';
control = #0..#31;
extended = #128..#255;

[handwritten note: what are these subranges of? maybe the standard stuff PASCAL knows about — numbers & characters]

To define an enumerated subrange, you must first define the enumerated data type. For example, the following enumerated subranges could be defined from the enumerated data type **computer = (IBM, Tandy, Dell, Commodore, Apple);**:

ibm_and_compats = IBM..Dell;
non_ibm = Commodore..Apple;

[handwritten note: these are enumerated subranges]

Listing 6.6 demonstrates how subranges are used in an actual Pascal program.

Listing 6.6

```
{ list6-6.pas - Demonstrate Pascal subrange data types }
program subranges;

type
     dice = 1..6;

var
     die1, die2 : dice;

begin
     randomize;
     repeat
          die1 := random(6) + 1;
          die2 := random(6) + 1;
          writeln('die1 = ', die1);
          writeln('die2 = ', die2);
     until die1 = die2;
end.
```

[handwritten note: If random(6)+1 = 4, does this mean die1 is the 4th element of the data type "dice"]

Listing 6.6 creates a subrange data type that can represent all of the legal values on a die. The program demonstrates this data type by assigning randomly generated rolls until two **dice** variables are equal (the program will keep rolling the dice until doubles come up).

LESSON 55. Sets

Many Pascal programs are required to handle data that doesn't seem to have a particular order to it. To deal with this, Pascal provides a user-defined data type called a **set**. A Pascal set is made up of either all of the members of an ordinal data type or a subrange of an ordinal data type. It cannot represent more than 256 distinct values. Consequently, only subranges can be used to define sets of **Words**, **Integers**, and **LongInts**. Figure 6-7 defines a Pascal set.

The following examples illustrate valid Pascal set definitions:

> **digits = set of '0'..'9';**
> **logical = set of boolean;**
> **lower_case = set of 'a'..'z';**

Figure 6-8 defines the format for assigning values to set variables and typed constants.

The following examples illustrate valid Pascal set assignment statements:

> **vowels := ['A', 'E', 'I', 'O', 'U'];**
> **seta := [1, 4, 6, 7, 9, 10];**
> **setb := [1, 4, 5...9, 100, 201];**

do you do both or Reuse for pesame set?

---

type
        identifier **= set of** ordinal data type;

Where:

identifier	is the data type's identifier.
ordinal data type	is an ordinal data type or subrange.

Figure 6-7. Defining a Pascal set.

```
identifier := [element list];

Where:
        identifier                  is the variable or typed constant identifier.

        element list                is a list of individual values, subranges, or
                                    both. Multiple elements are separated by
                                    commas.
```

Figure 6-8. Set assignments.

Pascal provides a variety of set-related operators to deal with sets. The remainder of this chapter is devoted to studying how these Pascal set operators function.

LESSON 56. The Set Equal to Operator

Like the normal Pascal equal to operator, the set equal to operator (=) compares two set expressions to see if they are equal. If the two set expressions are equal, the set equal to operator returns a value of **True**. Otherwise, the set equal to operator returns value of **False**. Figure 6-9 defines the set equal to operator.

```
set expression  =  set expression

Where:
        expression                  is a valid Pascal expression.
```

Figure 6-9. The Pascal set equal to operator.

Listing 6.7 demonstrates how the Pascal set equal to operator is used in an actual program.

Listing 6.7

```
{ list6-7.pas - Demonstrate the Pascal set equals operator }
program set_equals;

type
      characters = set of char;
```
continued...

111

...from previous page

```
var
      set1, set2, set3 : characters;

begin
      set1 := ['a'..'z'];
      set2 := ['A'..'Z'];
      set3 := set1;
      writeln('set1 = set2 is ', set1 = set2);
      writeln('set1 = set3 is ', set1 = set3);
end.
```

LESSON 57. The Set Not Equal to Operator

The Pascal set not equal to operator (<>) compares two set expressions to see if they are unequal in value. If the two set expressions aren't equal in value, the set not equal to operator returns a value of **True**. Otherwise, the set not equal to operator returns a value of **False**. Figure 6-10 defines the set not equal to operator.

set expression <> set expression

Where:
       set expression   is a valid Pascal set expression.

Figure 6-10. The Pascal set not equal to operator.

Listing 6.8 demonstrates how the Pascal set not equal to operator is used in an actual program.

Listing 6.8

```
{ list6-8.pas - Demonstrate the Pascal set does not equal operator }
program set_do_not_equal;

type
      characters = set of char;
```
continued...

...from previous page

```
var
      set1, set2, set3 : characters;

begin
      set1 := ['a'..'z'];
      set2 := ['A'..'Z'];
      set3 := set1;
      writeln('set1 <> set2 is ', set1 <> set2);
      writeln('set1 <> set3 is ', set1 <> set3);
end.
```

LESSON 58. The Set Less Than or Equal to Operator

The Pascal set less than or equal to operator (<=) compares two set expressions to see if all of the elements of the first set expression are in the second set expression. If the second set expression has at least all of the elements contained in the first set expression, the set less than or equal to operator returns a value of **True**. Otherwise, the set less than or equal to operator returns a value of **False**. Figure 6-11 defines the structure of the set less than or equal to operator.

---

set expression <= set expression

Where:
        set expression   is a valid Pascal set expression.

Figure 6-11. The Pascal set less than or equal to operator.

Listing 6.9 demonstrates how the Pascal set less than or equal to operator is used in an actual program.

Listing 6.9

```
{ list6-9.pas - Demonstrate the Pascal set less than or
equal to operator }
program set_less_than_or_equal;

type
      characters = set of char;
```
continued...

...from previous page
```
var
      set1, set2, set3 : characters;

begin
      set1 := ['a'..'z', 'A'..'Z'];
      set2 := ['A'..'Z'];
      set3 := ['a'..'z', #13];
      writeln('set2 <= set1 is ', set2 <= set1);
      writeln('set3 <= set1 is ', set3 <= set1);
end.
```

LESSON 59. The Set Greater Than or Equal to Operator

The Pascal set greater than or equal to operator (>=) compares two set expressions to see if all of the elements of the second set expression are in the first set expression. If the first set expression has at least all of the elements contained in the second set expression, the set greater than or equal to operator returns a value of **True**. Otherwise, the set greater than or equal to operator returns a value of **False**. Figure 6-12 defines the set greater than or equal to operator.

---

set expression >= set expression

Where:
          set expression   is a valid Pascal set expression.

Figure 6-12. The Pascal set greater than or equal to operator.

Listing 6.10 demonstrates how the Pascal set greater than or equal to operator is used in an actual program.

Listing 6.10

```
{ list6-10.pas - Demonstrate the Pascal set greater than
or equal to operator }
program set_greater_than_or_equal;
```
    continued...

...from previous page
```
type
      characters = set of char;

var
      set1, set2, set3 : characters;

begin
      set1 := ['a'..'z', 'A'..'Z'];
      set2 := ['A'..'Z'];
      set3 := ['a'..'z', #13];
      writeln('set2 >= set1 is ', set2 <= set1);
      writeln('set3 >= set1 is ', set3 <= set1);
end.
```

LESSON 60. The Set In Operator

The Pascal set **in** operator tests to see if the result of an ordinal expression is an element of a set expression. If the ordinal value is contained in the set, the set **in** operator returns a value of **True**. Otherwise, the set **in** operator returns a value of **False**. Figure 6-13 defines the set **in** operator.

---

ordinal expression **in** set expression

Where:

ordinal expression	is a valid Pascal ordinal expression.
set expression	is a valid Pascal set expression.

Figure 6-13. The Pascal in operator.

Listing 6.11 demonstrates how the Pascal set **in** operator is used in an actual program.

Listing 6.11

```
{ list6-11.pas - Demonstrate the Pascal in operator }
program in_demo;
```
continued...

...from previous page

```
procedure check_vowels(c : char);
const
      vowels : set of char = ['A', 'E', 'I', 'O', 'U',
                              'a', 'e', 'i', 'o', 'u' ];

begin
      if (c = 'Y') or (c = 'y') then
            writeln('Y is sometimes a vowel')
      else
            if c in vowels then
                    writeln(c, ' is a vowel')
            else
                    writeln(c, ' is a consonant');
end;

begin
      check_vowels('a');
      check_vowels('z');
      check_vowels('Y');
end.
```

LESSON 61. The Set Union Operator

The Pascal set union operator (+) returns the result of combining the elements of one set expression with the elements of another set expression. Figure 6-14 defines the set union operator.

Listing 6.12 demonstrates how the Pascal set union operator is used in an actual program.

---

set expression + set expression

Where:

      set expression   is a valid Pascal set expression.

Figure 6-14. The Pascal set union operator.

Listing 6.12

```
{ list6-12.pas - Demonstrate the Pascal set union operator }
program set_union_demo;

type
     digits = set of '0'..'9';

var
     set1, set2 : digits;

begin
     set1 := ['0'..'2'];
     set2 := ['4'..'9'] + set1;
     writeln('''1'' in set2 = ', '1' in set2);
     writeln('''3'' in set2 = ', '3' in set2);
     writeln('''5'' in set2 = ', '5' in set2);
end.
```

LESSON 62. The Set Difference Operator

The Pascal set difference operator (-) returns the result of removing the elements of a second set expression from a first set expression. Figure 6-15 defines the set difference operator.

Listing 6.13 demonstrates how the Pascal set difference operator is used in an actual program.

set expression - set expression

Where:
    set expression   is a valid Pascal set expression.

Figure 6-15. The Pascal set difference operator.

117

Listing 6.13

```
{ list6-13.pas - Demonstrate the Pascal set difference operator }
program set_difference_demo;

type
    digits = set of '0'..'9';

var
    set1, set2 : digits;

begin
    set1 := ['0'..'2'];
    set2 := ['0'..'9'] - set1;
    writeln('''1'' in set2 = ', '1' in set2);
    writeln('''3'' in set2 = ', '3' in set2);
    writeln('''5'' in set2 = ', '5' in set2);
end.
```

LESSON 63. The Set Intersection Operator

The Pascal set intersection operator (*) returns a set that is constructed from the elements that are common to two set expressions. Figure 6-16 defines the set intersection operator.

Listing 6.14 demonstrates how the Pascal set intersection operator is used in an actual program.

---

set expression * set expression

Where:

      set expression   is a valid Pascal set expression.

Figure 6-16. The Pascal set intersection operator.

118

Listing 6.14

```
{ list6-14.pas - Demonstrate the Pascal set intersection operator }
program set_intersection_demo;

type
     digits = set of '0'..'9';
var
     set1, set2 : digits;

begin
     set1 := ['0'..'3'];
     set2 := ['2'..'9'] * set1;
     writeln('''1'' in set2 = ', '1' in set2);
     writeln('''3'' in set2 = ', '3' in set2);
     writeln('''5'' in set2 = ', '5' in set2);
end.
```

***

You now know how to use various procedures, functions, and operators to define your own data types, and you are familiar with the concepts of subranges and sets. Chapter 7 teaches you how to join many items of the same data type under one identifier name.

Chapter **7**

Arrays

A lthough data types differ from each other a great deal, they all share one key
characteristic: they can only represent one piece of data at a time. This
chapter demonstrates how you can join numerous data items of the same
type under one identifier name by declaring the identifier to be an **array**. It discusses
simple, typed constant, and multi-dimensional arrays and tells you how to pass
arrays to procedures and functions.

LESSON 64. A Simple Array

Look at Listing 7.1. This program demonstrates how a student's grades could be
stored in ten integer variables. After safely tucking away the student's grades in the
variables, the program figures the sum of all the grades and uses the result to figure
the student's grade average.

Listing 7.1

```
{ list7-1.pas - Figure student's average no. 1 }
program stud_avg_1;

var
      g1, g2, g3, g4, g5, g6, g7, g8, g9, g10 : integer;
      total, ave : integer;

begin
      g1 := 90;
      g2 := 89;
      g3 := 100;
      g4 := 97;
      g5 := 85;
      g6 := 99;
      g7 := 96;
      g8 := 100;
      g9 := 94;
      g10 := 100;
      total := g1;
      total := total + g2;
      total := total + g3;
      total := total + g4;
      total := total + g5;
      total := total + g6;
      total := total + g7;
      total := total + g8;
      total := total + g9;
      total := total + g10;
      ave := total div 10;
      writeln('The student''s grade for the course is: ', ave);
end.
```

Although Listing 7.1 gets the job done, it is inefficient. To begin with, the program needs to declare each of the grade variables individually. An array, on the other hand, uses only one identifier for all of its individual elements. Figure 7-1 defines the structure for declaring an array.

```
        var
                identifier : array[index type] of data type;

        Where:
                identifier              is a valid Pascal identifier.

                index type              is an ordinal data type or ordinal subrange,
                                        except LongInt or LongInt must be
                                        subranges.

                data type               is the array's data type.
```

Figure 7-1. Declaring a Pascal array.

The number of elements in an array is defined by either an ordinal data type or subrange. Almost all array indexes are declared using subranges. The following are some examples of valid array declarations:

> **monthly_income : array[1..12] of real;**
> **temperatures : array[-200..200] of integer;**

If you want to declare an array for the grades in Listing 7.1, use something like the following:

> **g : array[1..10] of integer;**

Declaring the needed variables as an array is preferable to declaring them as individual variables. However, one problem remains. How are the individual elements of an array accessed? Fortunately, the method for accessing a Pascal array element is simple.

Figure 7-2 defines the structure for accessing an array element. The grades for the above example can be accessed as **g[1]**, **g[2]**, **g[3]**, **g[4]**, **g[5]**, **g[6]**, **g[7]**, **g[8]**, **g[9]**, and **g[10]**. Furthermore, operations can be performed on these individual array elements just as they would be on individually declared integer variables.

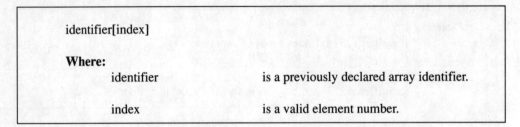

Figure 7-2. Accessing a Pascal array element.

Listing 7.2 presents a modified version of Listing 7.1. It substitutes an integer array for the student's grades. Besides showing how much easier it is to declare an array than numerous individual variables, Listing 7.2 also demonstrates how the student's total grade can be figured much more efficiently with a **for** loop. To accomplish this calculation, the program simply uses the loop counter **i** for the array element index. Thus, each of the array's individual elements are added together to form the total.

Listing 7.2

```
{ list7-2.pas - Figure student's average no. 2 }
program stud_avg_2;

var
      grades : array[1..10] of integer;
      i, total, ave : integer;

begin
      grades[1]  := 90;
      grades[2]  := 89;
      grades[3]  := 100;
      grades[4]  := 97;
      grades[5]  := 85;
      grades[6]  := 99;
      grades[7]  := 96;
      grades[8]  := 100;
      grades[9]  := 94;
      grades[10] := 100;
      total := 0;
```
continued...

...from previous page

```
for i := 1 to 10 do
      total := total + grades[i];
ave := total div 10;
writeln('The student''s grade for the course is: ', ave);
end.
```

LESSON 65.   Typed Constant Arrays

Although Listing 7.2 is an improvement over Listing 7.1, it could be simplified even further by declaring the student's grade array as a typed constant array. Figure 7.3 defines the structure for declaring a typed constant array. As shown in the figure, you declare typed constant array's initial values by surrounding them with parentheses and separating them with commas.

range of values

const
    identifier : **array**[index type] **of** data type = (initial values);

Where:

identifier	is a valid Pascal identifier.
index type	is an ordinal data type or an ordinal subrange, except **LongInt** or **LongInt** must be subranges.
data type	is the array's data type.
initial values	are the array elements' initial values, each of which is separated by a comma.

Figure 7-3. Declaring a typed constant array.

The following examples illustrate valid typed constant array declarations:

    vowels : array[1..5] of char = ('a', 'e', 'i', 'o', 'u');
    odd_numbers : array[1..5] of integer = (1, 3, 5, 7, 9);

Listing 7.3 demonstrates how you could modify Listing 7.2 even further by declaring the student's grade array as a typed constant. Even a cursory examination of the

125

program will disclose that the use of a typed constant array eliminates almost all of the assignment statements found in Listing 7.2.

Listing 7.3

```
{ list7-3.pas - Figure student's average no. 3 }
program stud_avg_3;

const
      grades : array[1..10] of integer = (90, 89, 100, 97,
      85, 99, 96, 100, 94, 100);

var
      i, total, ave : integer;

begin
      total := 0;
      for i := 1 to 10 do
           total := total + grades[i];
      ave := total div 10;
      writeln('The student''s grade for the course is: ', ave);
end.
```

LESSON 66. Multi-Dimensional Arrays

Although the programs already presented in this chapter have been useful for demonstrating how arrays are used in Pascal, they are not practical. These programs have demonstrated how a student's course average could be figured by totaling the student's scores and then figuring the average score. It is very unlikely, however, that a class would ever have just one student. Consequently, a useful program would have to be written in such a way that it could figure the course averages for a number of students. Listing 7.4 presents such a variation.

Listing 7.4

```
{ list7-4.pas - Figure student's average no. 4 }
program stud_avg_4;
```
  continued...

...from previous page

```
type
      grade_arr = array[1..10] of integer;

const
      student1 : grade_arr = (90, 89, 100, 97, 85, 99, 96,
                 100, 94, 100);
      student2 : grade_arr = (85, 75, 90, 88, 87, 93, 95,
                 97, 99, 100);

var
      i, total1, ave1, total2, ave2 : integer;

begin
      total1 := 0;
      total2 := 0;
      for i := 1 to 10 do
      begin
            total1 := total1 + student1[i];
            total2 := total2 + student2[i];
      end;
      ave1 := total1 div 10;
      ave2 := total2 div 10;
      writeln('Student no. 1''s grade for the course is:
      ', ave1);
      writeln('Student no. 2''s grade for the course is:
      ', ave2);
end.
```

Listing 7.4 declares a typed constant array for each of the students in the course. Although the program is functionally correct, it is far from being the most efficient Pascal program. A more efficient method for representing Listing 7.4 data would be to define it as a multi-dimensional array. Figure 7-4 defines the format for declaring a multi-dimensional array. Figure 7-5 defines the declaration of a multi-dimensional typed constant. Although these figures both show how a two-dimensional array is declared, multi-dimensional Pascal arrays are by no means limited to only two dimensions: three-dimensional arrays are common in a wide variety of programs.

var
        identifier **:** **array**[index type, index type] **of** data type;

Where:

identifier	is a valid Pascal identifier.
index type	is an ordinal data type or an ordinal subrange, except **LongInt** or **LongInt** must be subranges. The array's dimensional index types are separated by commas.
data type	is the array's data type.

Figure 7-4. Declaring a multi-dimensional array.

const
        identifier **:** **array**[index type, index type] **of** data type =
            ((initial values)**,** (initial values));

Where:

identifier	is a valid Pascal identifier.
index type	is an ordinal data type or an ordinal subrange, except **LongInt** or **LongInt** must be subranges. The array's dimensional index types are separated by commas.
data type	is the array's data type.
initial values	are the array elements' initial values, each of which is separated by a comma.

Figure 7-5. Declaring a multi-dimensional typed constant.

Accessing a multi-dimensional array element is slightly different from accessing a single-dimensional array element. Figure 7-6 defines two methods for accessing a multi-dimensional array element. Although both methods are acceptable, the first method is preferred.

```
        identifier[index, index]

               or

        identifier[index] [index]
```

Where:

identifier   is a previously declared array identifier.

index   is a valid element number.

Figure 7-6. Accessing a multi-dimensional array element.

Listing 7.5 presents a slightly modified version of Listing 7.4. It substitutes a multi-dimensional typed constant array for the two individual student arrays.

Listing 7.5

```pascal
{ list7-5.pas - Figure student's average no. 5 }
program stud_avg_5;
const
     students : array[1..2, 1..10] of integer =
          ( (90, 89, 100, 97, 85, 99, 96, 100, 94, 100),
            (85, 75, 90, 88, 87, 93, 95, 97, 99, 100) );

var
     i, total1, total2, ave1, ave2 : integer;

begin
     total1 := 0;
     total2 := 0;
     for i := 1 to 10 do
     begin
          total1 := total1 + students[1, i];
          total2 := total2 + students[2, i];
     end;
     ave1 := total1 div 10;
```
...continued

...from previous page

```
        ave2 := total2 div 10;
        writeln('Student no. 1''s grade for the course is:
        ', ave1);
        writeln('Student no. 2''s grade for the course is:
        ', ave2);
end.
```

Although Listing 7.5 is a step in the right direction, it is wasteful to use four variables to figure the two students' course averages.

Listing 7.6 demonstrates an even simpler version of the program; it uses a nested **for** loop to calculate the course averages.

Listing 7.6

```
{ list7-6.pas - Figure student's average no. 6 }
program stud_avg_6;
const
        students : array[1..2, 1..10] of integer =
                ( (90, 89, 100, 97, 85, 99, 96, 100, 94, 100),
                (85, 75, 90, 88, 87, 93, 95, 97, 99, 100) );

var
        i, j, total, ave : integer;

begin
        for i := 1 to 2 do
        begin
                total := 0;
                for j := 1 to 10 do
                begin
                        total := total + students[i, j];
                end;
                ave := total div 10;
                writeln('Student no. ', i, '''s grade for the
                course is: ', ave);
        end;
end.
```

LESSON 67.   Passing Arrays to Procedures and Functions

To pass an array to a procedure or a function, you first define a data type for the array. Note that the one exception to this is for **strings**. **Strings** are nothing more than a **char** array. Because they are defined as part of the Pascal programming language, they are already a predefined data type.

Figure 7-7 defines the structure of an array data type. An array data type is defined like any other new data type; once it has been defined, it can be used to indicate an identifier's data type.

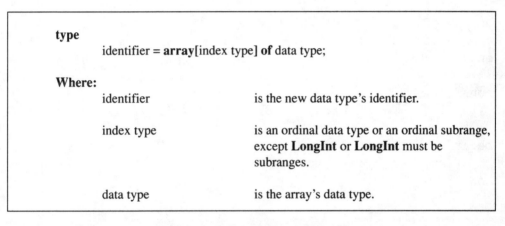

type

    identifier = **array**[index type] **of** data type;

Where:

    identifier   is the new data type's identifier.

    index type   is an ordinal data type or an ordinal subrange, except **LongInt** or **LongInt** must be subranges.

    data type   is the array's data type.

Figure 7-7. Defining an array data type.

Listing 7.7 demonstrates how an array is passed to a function in an actual Pascal program. Note that by using the **var** keyword in the **total** function's head, the array is passed by reference. Although arrays can be passed by value, Pascal has to make a temporary copy of the array before each procedure call. Not only is this a time-consuming process, it could easily consume all available memory. This is particularly true if the procedure or function is recursive. Consequently, it is usually best to pass arrays by reference instead of by value.

Listing 7.7

```
{ list7-7.pas - Demonstrate how an array is passed to a function }
program array_passing_demo;
```
    continued...

...from previous page

```
type
      list_array = array[1..10] of integer;

function total(var la : list_array) : integer;
var
      i, t : integer;

begin
      t := 0;
      for i := 1 to 10 do
            t := t + la[i];
      total := t;
end;

const
      list : list_array = (3, 2, 4, 5, 6, 7, 8, 9, 1, 9);

begin
      writeln('Total for the array is ', total(list));
end.
```

***

You now know how to group multiple data items of the same type in simple, typed constant, and multi-dimensional arrays, and how to pass arrays to procedures and functions. Chapter 8 tells you how to group data items of different types in a record.

Chapter 8

Records

Although arrays are a useful programming tool, many programs work with related data of different types. Pascal offers a user-defined data type called **records** that allows you to group data of different types. This chapter introduces you to **records** and discusses the **with** statement, typed constant records, and record and field arrays.

Before we examine the details of Pascal records, let's take a look at Listing 8.1. This program builds upon the programs presented in Chapter 7. Instead of just displaying the course averages, however, it also displays the students' names. The names and the averages are related data, but they are represented by vastly different data types.

Listing 8.1

```
{ list8-1.pas - Nonrecord demonstration }
program nonrecord;

var
      name1, name2 : string;
      ave1, ave2 : integer;

begin
      name1 := 'John Smith';
      ave1 := 95;
      name2 := 'Jane Doe';
      ave2 := 98;
      writeln(name1, '''s average is a ', ave1);
      writeln(name2, '''s average is a ', ave2);
end.
```

LESSON 68. Record Basics

The first step in using a record in a Pascal program is to define the record's data type. Figure 8-1 defines the structure for declaring a Pascal record. The record declaration is constructed from a number of field declarations.

```
      type
            data type identifier = record
                  field declaration;
                  .

                  .
                  field declaration;
            end;

      Where:
            data type identifier        is the new data type's identifier.

            field declaration           is a valid field declaration.
```

Figure 8-1. Declaring a Pascal record type.

Figure 8-2 defines a field declaration. Field declarations are similar to variable definitions.

The following examples illustrate valid Pascal record declarations:

```
mail_item = record
        name1, name2, address : string[30];
        city : string[15];
        state : string[2];
        zip1 : string[5];
        zip2 : string[4];
end;

student = record
        name : string;
        grades : array[1..10] of integer;
end;
```

Figure 8-3 defines a record variable's field reference in an assignment statement or an expression. You refer to the field by separating the variable's name and the field's name with a period (.).

---

field identifier : data type;

Where:

field identifier	is the record field's identifier.
data type	is the record field's data type.

Figure 8-2. Declaring a Pascal record field.

---

variable identifier.field identifier

Where:

variable identifier	is the record variable's name.
field identifier	is the field name.

Figure 8-3. Record variable field references.

The following are a few examples of valid Pascal record variable field references:

item.name1 := 'John Smith';
item.address := '375 Sleepy Lane';
s1.name := 'Jane Doe';
total := s1.grades[1] + s1.grades[2];

Listing 8.2 demonstrates how Listing 8.1 can be rewritten to take advantage of Pascal's support for record data types. Even though it is only a simple example of how Pascal record types are used in an actual program, it shows how related data can be joined together as a single entry, thereby eliminating the necessity of using separate variables for each field.

Listing 8.2

```
{ list8-2.pas - Record demonstration }
program record_demo;

type
      student = record
            name : string;
            ave : integer;
      end;

var
      s1, s2 : student;

begin
      s1.name := 'John Smith';
      s1.ave := 95;
      s2.name := 'Jane Doe';
      s2.ave := 98;
      writeln(s1.name, '''s average is a ', s1.ave);
      writeln(s2.name, '''s average is a ', s2.ave);
end.
```

LESSON 69. The With Statement

Although Pascal records are a valuable programming tool, records with long variable names are hard to work with because you must type the variable name before each of the field names. As an example, suppose you were to write a mail list program that uses a record type similar to the following:

```
list_item = record
        name, address : string[30];
        city : string[15];
        state : string[2];
        zip : string[5];
    end;
```

Now suppose that the program uses the following statements to assign values to a **list_item** record variable named **mail_list_item1**:

```
mail_list_item1.name := 'John Smith';
mail_list_item1.address := '325 Cherry Tree Lane';
mail_list_item1.city := 'Washington';
mail_list_item1.state := 'DC';
mail_list_item1.zip := '00001';
```

Typing **mail_list_item1** over and over is a tedious task. Wouldn't it be nice if there was a shorthand method for writing the above assignment statements? Pascal comes to the rescue with the **with** statement. Figure 8-4 defines the format for using the **with** statement to eliminate the necessity of having to retype the variables.

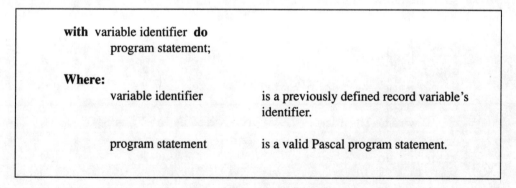

with variable identifier **do**	
program statement;	
Where:	
variable identifier	is a previously defined record variable's identifier.
program statement	is a valid Pascal program statement.

Figure 8-4. The Pascal with statement.

The following statements (which are simpler than the previous statements) show how the **with** statement can be used to rewrite the above **mail_list_item1** statements:

```
with mail_list_item1 do
begin
        name := 'John Smith';
        address := '325 Cherry Tree Lane';
        city := 'Washington';
        state := 'DC';
        zip := '00001';
end;
```

Listing 8.3 demonstrates how Listing 8.2 can be rewritten to take advantage of the Pascal **with** statement.

Listing 8.3

```
{ list8-3.pas - With statement demonstration }
program with_demo;

type
    student = record
        name : string;
        ave : integer;
    end;
var
    s1, s2 : student;

begin
    with s1 do
    begin
        name := 'John Smith';
        ave := 95;
        writeln(name, '''s average is a ', ave);
    end;
    with s2 do

    begin
```
continued...

...from previous page

```
        name := 'Jane Doe';
            ave := 98;
            writeln(name, '''s average is a ', ave);
        end;
end.
```

LESSON 70. Typed Constant Records

Like arrays, Pascal records can be declared as typed constants to furnish an easy way
for providing records with initial values. Figure 8-5 defines the declaration of a typed
constant record. You initialize a typed constant by specifying initial values for the
record variable's fields.

The following are some examples of valid typed constant record definitions:

> **list1 : mail = (name : 'John Smith'; address : '338 Main St.**
> **Suite C'; city : 'Somewhere'; state : 'US'; zip : '00000');**
> **s1 : student = (name : 'Jane Doe'; grade : 99);**

Listing 8.4 demonstrates how Listing 8.2 can be further modified to utilize typed
constant records. The use of typed constant records in Listing 8.4 greatly simplifies
the program.

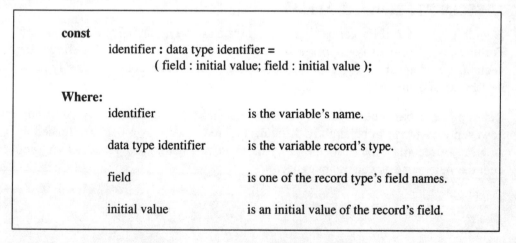

const		
	identifier : data type identifier =	
	(field : initial value; field : initial value);	
Where:		
	identifier	is the variable's name.
	data type identifier	is the variable record's type.
	field	is one of the record type's field names.
	initial value	is an initial value of the record's field.

Figure 8-5. Declaring a typed constant record.

Listing 8.4

```
{ list8-4.pas - Typed constant record demonstration }
program type_const_record_demo;

type
     student = record
          name : string;
          ave : integer;
     end;

const
     s1 : student = (name : 'John Smith'; ave : 95);
     s2 : student = (name : 'Jane Doe'; ave : 98);

begin
     Writeln(s1.name, '''s average is a ', s1.ave);
     Writeln(s2.name, '''s average is a ', s2.ave);
end.
```

LESSON 71. Record Arrays

Wouldn't it be nice if Pascal used record arrays and arrays for fields in a program? Fortunately, Pascal fully supports both types of arrays. Figure 8-6 defines the declaration of an array of records. There is no difference between this type of declaration and any other array declaration.

Referencing a particular record field while using record arrays in a program, however, may prove to be slightly difficult. Figure 8-7 defines a field referenced in an array of records. Note how the array index comes before the period (.) and not after the field name as you might expect.

```
      var
              identifier : array[index type] of record type;

  Where:
              identifier                    is a valid Pascal identifier.

              index type                    is an ordinal data type or ordinal subrange,
                                            except LongInt or LongInt must be
                                            subranges.

              record type                   is a previously defined record type.
```

Figure 8-6. Declaring an array of records.

```
  variable identifier[index].field identifier;

  Where:
              variable identifier           is the record variable's name.

              index                         is the record array's element number.

              field identifier              is the field name.
```

Figure 8-7. Record array field references.

Listing 8.5 demonstrates a variation of earlier programs in this chapter. It utilizes a record array to store the student data.

Listing 8.5

```
{ list8-5.pas - Demonstrate record arrays }
program record_arrays;

type
     student = record
          name : string;
continued...
```

...from previous page

```
            ave : integer;
      end;

const
      class : array[1..2] of student =
            ( (name : 'John Smith'; ave : 95),
              (name : 'Jane Doe'; ave : 98) );

begin
      writeln(class[1].name, '''s average is a ',
      class[1].ave);
      writeln(class[2].name, '''s average is a ',
      class[2].ave);
end.
```

LESSON 72. Field Arrays

Figure 8-8 defines the declaration of a field array. This procedure is the same as any other array declaration. Figure 8-9 shows the proper method for referencing a field element. You specify the field element's array index immmediately after the field's name.

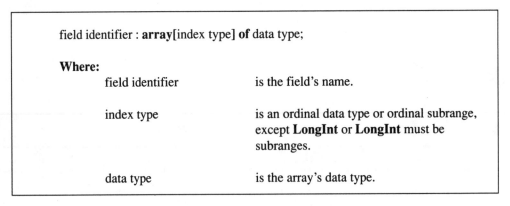

field identifier : **array**[index type] **of** data type;

Where:

field identifier	is the field's name.
index type	is an ordinal data type or ordinal subrange, except **LongInt** or **LongInt** must be subranges.
data type	is the array's data type.

Figure 8-8. Declaring a field array.

variable identifier.field identifier[index]

Where:

variable identifier	is the record variable's name.
field identifier	is the record field's name.
index	is the field array's element number.

Figure 8-9. Field array references.

Listing 8.6 demonstrates how the programs in this chapter and the last chapter can be rewritten to take advantage of field arrays. Listing 8.6 is the superior program, as it fully integrates all of the related student data into one neat record array.

Listing 8.6

```
{ list8-6.pas - Demonstrate array fields }
program record_arrays;

type
     student = record
          name : string;
          grades : array[1..10] of integer;
     end;

const
     class : array[1..2] of student =
          ( (name : 'John Smith';grades : ( 90, 89, 100,
             97, 85, 99, 96, 100, 94, 100) ),
            (name : 'Jane Doe'; grades : ( 85, 75, 90,
             88, 87, 93, 95, 97, 99, 100) ) );

var
     i, j, total, ave : integer;
```
continued...

143

...from previous page

```
begin
      for i := 1 to 2 do
      begin
            total := 0;
            for j := 1 to 10 do
                  total := total + class[i].grades[j];
            ave := total div 10;
            writeln(class[i].name, '''s average is a ', ave);
      end;
end.
```

***

You now understand the concept of records and are familiar with the **with** statement, typed constant records, and record and field arrays. Chapter 9 discusses variant records—records that can vary their fields depending on the data type to be stored.

Chapter 9

Variant Records

This chapter examines the **variant record**. As its name implies, the variant record is able to vary its fields depending on the type of data to be stored. Although the concept of variant records may sound strange, this type of record can be a useful and powerful programming tool.

LESSON 73. Variant Record Basics

To better understand the power of Pascal variant records, first take a look at Listing 9.1. This program demonstrates a short faculty/student list for a small college. The distinguishing feature of this program is its need for two record types: one for a faculty member and one for a member of the student body. Obviously, a record for a faculty member needs different data than a record for a student.

Listing 9.1

```
{ list9-1.pas - Display faculty/student list without variant records}
program disp_list1;

type
      class_type = ( freshman, sophomore, junior, senior );
      faculty = record
            name : string;
            age : integer;
            salary : real;
            years : integer;
      end;
      student = record
            name : string;
            age : integer;
            average : real;
            class : class_type;
      end;

const
      f_list : array[1..2] of faculty =
            ( (name : 'John Smith'; age : 53; salary : 33500;
               years : 15),
              (name : 'Jane Doe'; age : 45; salary : 33500;
               years : 14) );
      s_list : array[1..2] of student =
            ( (name : 'Calvin Doe'; age : 20; average : 3.76;
               class : junior),
              (name : 'Sue Smith'; age : 22; average : 4.0;
               class : senior) );

var
      i : integer;

begin
      for i := 1 to 2 do
            with f_list[i] do
```
continued...

...from previous page

```
                writeln(name, ' ', age, ' ', salary:8:2, ' ',
                years);
    for i := 1 to 2 do
        with s_list[i] do
        begin
                write(name, ' ', age, ' ', average:4:2, ' ');
                case class of
                        freshman : writeln('Freshman');
                        sophomore : writeln('Sophomore');
                        junior : writeln('Junior');
                        senior : writeln('Senior');
                end;
        end;
end.
```

Although the above program gets the job done, wouldn't it be nice if the faculty and student records could be combined into one record type? Look at the following example:

```
fs_rec = record
        name : string;
        age : integer;
        salary : real;
        years : integer;
        average : real;
        class : class_type;
    end;
```

The above record type would work, but it would waste an enormous amount of space. After all, you wouldn't need to store a grade point average or class for a faculty member or a salary or number of years employed for a student. This type of data handling requirement is ideally suited for a variant record. Not only can the two record types be combined, but a variant record requires only as much memory as the largest individual record from which it is constructed. Figure 9-1 defines the declaration of a variant record.

```
record identifier = record
        field declaration;
        .
        .
        field declaration;
        case tag identifier : data type of
                case label : ( field declaration; );
                .
                .
                case label : ( field declaration; );
        end;
```

Where:

record identifier	is the data type's identifier.
field declaration	is a valid field declaration. Multiple fields in the variant **case..end** structure must be separated by a semicolon.
tag identifier	is an optional tag identifier. If used, the "case" can be accessed through the tag identifier just as it is with any other field.
data type	is the tag identifier's data type.
case label	is a label that identifies which field the variant records will use for a particular tag.

Figure 9-1. Declaring a variant record.

Listing 9.2 demonstrates how you can modify Listing 9.1 to take advantage of Pascal's variant records. The main feature of this program is its use of the tag identifier **fs** in the **fs_rec** variant record type. With this record field set to indicate the type of data stored in the variant record, it is an easy task to extract and properly display each of the variant record's appropriate values. Without **fs**, it would be impossible to know what type of data is stored in the variant record and how it is properly handled.

Listing 9.2

```
{ list9-2.pas - Display faculty/student list with variant records}
program disp_list1;

type
     fs_type = ( faculty, student );
     class_type = ( freshman, sophomore, junior, senior );
     fs_rec = record
             name : string;
             age : integer;
             case fs : fs_type of
                     faculty : ( salary : real; years : integer; );
                     student : ( average : real; class : class_type);
     end;

const
     list : array[1..4] of fs_rec =
             ( (name : 'John Smith'; age : 53; fs : faculty;
               salary : 33500; years : 15),
               (name : 'Jane Doe'; age : 45; fs : faculty;
               salary : 33500; years : 14),
               (name : 'Calvin Doe'; age : 20; fs : student;
               average : 3.76; class : junior),
               (name : 'Sue Smith'; age : 22; fs : student;
               average : 4.0; class : senior) );

var
     i : integer;

begin
     for i := 1 to 4 do
             with list[i] do
                     if fs = faculty then
                             writeln(name, ' ', age, ' ',
                             salary:8:2, ' ', years)
                     else
                     begin
```
continued...

...from previous page

```
                    write(name, ' ', age, ' ',
                    average:4:2, ' ');
                    case class of
                            freshman : writeln('Freshman');
                            sophomore : writeln('Sophomore');
                            junior : writeln('Junior');
                            senior : writeln('Senior');
                    end;
              end;
end.
```

***

You now know how to use variant records. Chapter 10 introduces you to pointers.

Chapter 10

Pointers

This chapter examines simple array/record, and procedure/function pointers. Pointers "point" to a data value of a specific type. For example, an **integer** pointer points to an **integer** value, a **real** pointer points to a **real** value, etc. In addition to pointing to data values, a pointer can also point to a procedure or a function. Although they may not sound terribly important, pointers are one of Pascal's most significant features. Consequently, you should be well acquainted with how pointers are declared and how they are used in programs.

LESSON 74. Simple Pointers

As with all other types of data, a Pascal pointer must be declared before it is used in a program. Figure 10-1 defines the declaration of a Pascal pointer.

```
    var
            identifier : ^data type;

Where:
            identifier                    is the pointer's identifier.

            data type                     is the data type to which the pointer points.
```

Figure 10-1. Declaring a Pascal pointer.

The following examples illustrate valid pointer declarations:

int1ptr, int2ptr : ^integer;
nameptr : ^string;
AmountPtr : ^Real;

Note that a pointer declaration is much like a normal variable declaration: there is no initial value assigned to the pointer. Therefore, results will be unpredictable if you use a pointer without first initializing it. You can initialize a pointer by assigning it an address of the proper data type, assigning it the value of another pointer of the same data type, or assigning it the special value **nil**.

The format for assigning a pointer the value of an address of a data value is defined in Figure 10-2. As this figure shows, you can use either the Pascal (**@**) operator or **addr** function to assign the address of the data value to the pointer. Since both methods perform the same task, it doesn't matter which method you use.

```
    pointer identifier := @variable identifier;
        or
    pointer identifier := addr(variable identifier);

Where:
            pointer identifier            is the pointer's identifier.

            variable identifier           is the identifier of the variable whose address
                                          will be assigned to the pointer. Note: Both
                                          variable identifier and pointer identifier must
                                          be of the same type.
```

Figure 10-2. Assigning a variable's address to a pointer.

Figure 10-3 shows the format for assigning the value of one pointer to another. Assigning one pointer to another is like assigning the value of one variable to another.

Figure 10-4 defines the process of assigning the value **nil** to a pointer. The value **nil** is used to indicate a pointer that has no special meaning. It's usually a good idea to set a pointer that doesn't have a meaning to **nil**. That way, the program can check for a **nil** pointer before it carries out a meaningless operation on an unassigned pointer.

Although all of this material about pointers is interesting, you're probably wondering how the data value to which a pointer is pointing is actually accessed. It's simple: you add a (^) to the end of the pointer's identifier. This tells Pascal to treat the pointer identifier as a variable identifier for the data value to which it points. The following are a few examples of pointers being used to retrieve and store data values:

> **int_ptr^ := 35 div count;**
> **int_result := int_ptr^ + 5;**

Listing 10.1 demonstrates how Pascal pointers are declared and used in an actual program.

---

pointer identifier := pointer identifier;

Where:

       pointer identifier   is a previously declared pointer identifier.

Figure 10-3. Assigning the value of one pointer to another.

---

pointer identifier := **nil**;

Where:

       pointer identifier   is a previously declared pointer identifier.

Figure 10-4. Assigning nil to a pointer.

Listing 10.1

```
{ list10-1.pas - Simple pointers demo }
program simple_pointers;

var
      intptr : ^integer;
      i1, i2 : integer;

begin
      i1 := 1;
      i2 := 2;
      intptr := @i1;
      writeln('intptr^ is ', intptr^, ' and so isn''t ', i1);
      intptr^ := i2;
      writeln('Now intptr has changed i1 to ', i1);
end.
```

LESSON 75. Array and Record Pointers

Besides supporting pointers to simple variables, Pascal also supports array and record pointers. Figure 10-5 defines an array element referenced by an array pointer. Figure 10-6 defines a record field referenced by a record pointer. As with a simple variable reference, you specify a pointer reference to either an array element or a record field by putting a (^) after the pointer's identifier.

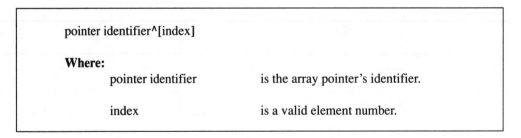

Figure 10-5 content:

pointer identifier^[index]

Where:
        pointer identifier   is the array pointer's identifier.

        index   is a valid element number.

Figure 10-5. Array pointer referencing.

```
┌─────────────────────────────────────────────────────────────────┐
│                                                                   │
│      pointer identifier^.field identifier                         │
│                                                                   │
│   Where:                                                          │
│           pointer identifier          is the record pointer's name. │
│                                                                   │
│           field identifier            is the field name.          │
│                                                                   │
└─────────────────────────────────────────────────────────────────┘
```

Figure 10-6. Record pointer referencing.

Listing 10.2 demonstrates how an array pointer is used in an actual Pascal program. This program initializes an array by using an array pointer to store the elements' values. Once stored, the appropriate values are displayed by accessing them with normal array element referencing methods.

Listing 10.2

```
{ list10-2.pas - Array pointers }
program array_pointers;

type
      intarray = array[1..10] of integer;

var
      iaptr : ^intarray;
      ia : intarray;
      i : integer;

begin
      iaptr := @ia;
      for i := 1 to 10 do
            iaptr^[i] := i;
      for i := 1 to 10 do
            writeln('ia[', i, '] = ', ia[i]);
end.
```

Listing 10.3 demonstrates how a record pointer is used in a Pascal program. Similar to Listing 10.2, this program initializes a record by using a record pointer to assign the initial values to the record's fields. Once the appropriate values are assigned, they are displayed by using the normal Pascal record field referencing methods.

Listing 10.3

```
{ list10-3.pas - Record pointers }
program record_pointers;

type
    maillist = record
        name, address, city, state, zip : string;
    end;

var
    mlptr : ^maillist;
    item : maillist;

begin
    mlptr := addr(item);
    mlptr^.name := 'John Smith';
    mlptr^.address := 'West 57th St.';
    mlptr^.city := 'Somewhere';
    mlptr^.state := 'US';
    mlptr^.zip := '00001';
    writeln('Name:    ', item.name);
    writeln('Address: ', item.address);
    writeln('City   : ', item.city);
    writeln('State  : ', item.state);
    writeln('Zip    : ', item.zip);
end.
```

LESSON 76. Procedure and Function Pointers

Now that you have explored how pointers can be used to manipulate simple variables, array variables, and records, you will learn how they can be used with procedures and functions. Before you continue with pointers, however, you need to understand procedure and function variables. A procedure or a function variable is a variable that can hold the address of a procedure or function. With the address safely tucked away in a variable, the appropriate procedure or function can be called by simply using the identifier in place of the name.

Suppose you were writing a program that required different routines to be called depending upon a variety of conditions. You could write a convoluted decision-making statement to handle the different circumstances, but it's much easier to modify a procedure or function variable when a certain condition occurs. That way, a single procedure or function call can handle any circumstance that might arise in a program.

To be able to declare a procedure or function variable in a program, you must first define a data type for the variable. Figure 10-7 illustrates the format for defining a procedure data type.

Figure 10-8 illustrates the format for defining a function data type. Basically, a data type is defined with a procedure or function head that doesn't have an identifier. Once you've defined an appropriate data type, you can declare a procedure or function variable just like any other variable: it can be declared as a simple variable, an array variable, a record field etc.

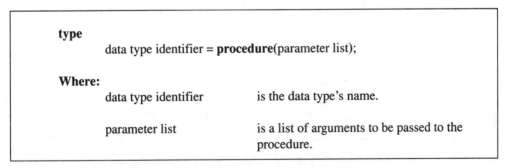

Figure 10-7. Defining a procedure data type.

---

type

data type identifier = **function**(parameter list) : return type;

Where:

data type identifier	is the data type's name.
parameter list	is a list of arguments to be passed to the function.
return type	is the return value's data type.

Figure 10-8. Defining a function data type.

Before you can use a variable to call a procedure or a function, you must assign an initial value to it. Figure 10-9 defines the assignment of an address to a variable. You must use an (**@**) operator before the procedure or function variable's name. Without the (**@**) operator, Pascal tries to execute the procedure or function contained in the variable, and attempting to call the routine in an unassigned procedure or function variable is unacceptable.

@variable identifier := @procedure identifier;
    or
@variable identifier := @function identifier;

Where:

variable identifier	is the procedure or function variable's name.
procedure identifier	is the procedure's name.
function identifier	is the function's name.

Figure 10-9. Procedure and function variable assignments.

Listing 10.4 demonstrates how procedure variables can be used in an actual program to build a simple menu system. Procedure and function variables can be quite effective for building a menu system. If a menu item needs to be changed, the new routine's address can be assigned to the appropriate procedure variable. This permits the program to quickly and efficiently modify itself due to a change in current conditions.

Listing 10.4

```
{ list10-4.pas - Procedure and function variables demo }
program proc_and_func_vars;

uses crt;
procedure m1;
begin
     writeln('This is menu item 1');
end;

procedure m2;
begin
     writeln('This is menu item 2');
end;

procedure m3;
begin
     writeln('This is menu item 3');
end;

procedure m4;
begin
     writeln('This is menu item 4');
end;

procedure m5;
begin
     halt;
end;

type
     proc = procedure;
```
continued...

...from previous page

```
var
      menuprocs : array[1..5] of proc;
      key : integer;

begin
      @menuprocs[1]  :=  @m1;
      @menuprocs[2]  :=  @m2;
      @menuprocs[3]  :=  @m3;
      @menuprocs[4]  :=  @m4;
      @menuprocs[5]  :=  @m5;
      while true do
      begin
            writeln('[1]...Menu Item # 1');
            writeln('[2]...Menu Item # 2');
            writeln('[3]...Menu Item # 3');
            writeln('[4]...Menu Item # 4');
            writeln('[5]...Exit The Program');
            repeat
                  key := integer(readkey);
            until (key > 48) and (key < 54);
            menuprocs[key - 48];
      end;
end.
```

Now that you know how to build a menu system using procedure variables, let's see how the same system could be built using pointers. To assign a procedure's or a function's address to a pointer, first define a pointer with a data type of **pointer**. A **pointer** pointer has no real data type and can hold a pointer for anything. Figure 10-10 defines the structure for declaring a **pointer** pointer. As shown in the figure, a **pointer** pointer is declared like any other pointer.

---

var
　　　pointer identifier **: pointer**;

Where:
　　　pointer identifier　　　　is the pointer's name.

Figure 10-10. Declaring a pointer pointer.

Figure 10-11 defines the structure for assigning a procedure's or a function's address to a **pointer**. Unlike procedure and function variable assignments, a **pointer** assignment doesn't require the (**@**) operator before the pointer's identifier. The address is being assigned to a generic pointer. Therefore, there is no way Pascal can confuse a pointer with a function call.

---

pointer identifier := @procedure identifier;
     or
pointer identifier := @function identifier;

Where:

pointer identifier	is the procedure or function pointer's name.
procedure identifier	is the procedure's name.
function identifier	is the function's name.

Figure 10-11. Assigning a procedure or function address to a pointer.

Listing 10.5 presents a modified version of Listing 10.4. It uses pointers instead of procedure variables to implement the menu system. A distinguising factor of this program is the use of typecasting to perform actual procedure calls. Without casting the pointer to a procedure call, Pascal would assume that an assignment statement was being constructed and would generate an unintended error.

Listing 10.5

```
{ list10-5.pas - Procedure and function pointers demo }
program proc_and_func_ptrs;

uses crt;

procedure m1;
begin
     writeln('This is menu item 1');
end;
```
   continued...

...from previous page

```
procedure m2;
begin
     writeln('This is menu item 2');
end;

procedure m3;
begin
     writeln('This is menu item 3');
end;

procedure m4;
begin
     writeln('This is menu item 4');
end;

procedure m5;
begin
     halt;
end;

type
     proc = procedure;

var
     menuprocs : array[1..5] of pointer;
     key : integer;

begin
     menuprocs[1] := @m1;
     menuprocs[2] := @m2;
     menuprocs[3] := @m3;
     menuprocs[4] := @m4;
     menuprocs[5] := @m5;
     while true do
     begin
          writeln('[1]...Menu Item # 1');
          writeln('[2]...Menu Item # 2');
```

continued...

...from previous page

```
            writeln('[3]...Menu Item # 3');
            writeln('[4]...Menu Item # 4');
            writeln('[5]...Exit The Program');
            repeat
                  key := integer(readkey);
            until (key > 48) and (key < 54);
            proc(menuprocs[key - 48]);
      end;
end.
```

***

You now know how to use pointers. Chapter 11 discusses dynamic memory management—one of the most important uses for Pascal pointers.

Chapter 11

Dynamic Memory Management

This chapter introduces one of the most important uses of Pascal pointers: dynamic memory management. It teaches you how to allocate and deallocate single data objects as well as blocks of memory. When the program is compiled, Pascal automatically sets aside a place in the computer's memory to store the variables' contents. Many times, however, you can't possibly know what a program's data requirements are until the program is actually run.

Pascal provides a number of useful dynamic memory management routines that allow you to write programs that can expand or contract their data space. You can use these routines to allocate and deallocate memory for either a single data object or an entire block of memory.

LESSON 77. Allocating and Deallocating Single Data Objects

You will begin your study of dynamic memory management by examining how single data objects are allocated and deallocated. To allocate a data object, you use the **new** procedure. Figure 11-1 defines this procedure. As shown in the figure, a pointer is passed as the **new** procedure's only argument. When the **new** procedure returns to the calling program, the pointer points to a memory location of the same size as the pointer's data type.

You use the **dispose** procedure to deallocate a previously allocated data object. Figure 11-2 defines the **dispose** procedure. Like the **new** procedure, the **dispose** procedure requires a single pointer argument. Essentially, the **dispose** procedure releases the pointer's previously allocated memory area. Once released, the deallocated memory area is available to be used by other dynamic memory management calls.

Listing 11.1 demonstrates how the **new** and **dispose** procedures are used to dynamically allocate and deallocate memory. The program allocates space for an integer data object, assigns a value to the data object, displays the data object's value, and releases the data object's allocated memory area. As you can see from this program, allocating and deallocating dynamic memory is simple.

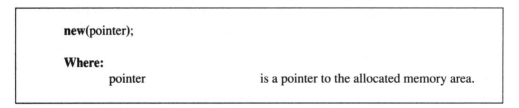

> **new**(pointer);
>
> **Where:**
>   pointer   is a pointer to the allocated memory area.

Figure 11-1. Allocating memory with the new procedure.

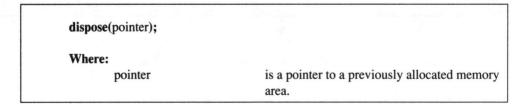

> **dispose**(pointer);
>
> **Where:**
>   pointer   is a pointer to a previously allocated memory area.

Figure 11-2. Deallocating memory with the dispose procedure.

Listing 11.1

```
{ list11-1.pas - Demonstrate allocating/deallocating a single object }
program alloc_dealloc;

var
    int_ptr : ^integer;

begin
    new(int_ptr);
    int_ptr^ := 4;
    writeln('int_ptr^ = ', int_ptr^);
    dispose(int_ptr);
end.
```

LESSON 78. Allocating and Deallocating Blocks of Memory

Allocating and deallocating a single data object is a very useful programming tool, except if you want to dynamically allocate and deallocate memory for an array that varies in size during the life of the program. To fill this need, Pascal provides the **getmem** and **freemem** procedures. As its name implies, the **getmem** procedure gets (or allocates) a block of dynamic memory. Figure 11-3 defines the getmem procedure. Like the **new** procedure, the **getmem** procedure requires a pointer argument to return a pointer to the allocated memory. The **getmem** procedure also requires that you specify the number of bytes to be allocated. The most convenient way to specify the number of allocation bytes is to use Pascal's **sizeof** function.

---

getmem(pointer, size);

Where:

        pointer   is a pointer to the allocated memory block.

        size   is the size of the memory block, in bytes.

Figure 11-3. Allocating a memory block with getmem.

167

Figure 11-4 defines the **sizeof** function. The **sizeof** function returns the size (in bytes) for any previously defined data type. Consequently, the number of bytes required for a 100 element integer array could be specified with the following expression:

100 * sizeof(integer)

As a compliment to the **getmem** procedure, the **freemem** procedure deallocates a previously allocated memory block. Figure 11-5 defines the **freemem** procedure. As with the **getmem** procedure, the **freemem** procedure requires that you use a pointer to the memory block and specify the size of the block, in bytes.

Listing 11.2 demonstrates how the Pascal **getmem** and **freemem** procedures are used to dynamically allocate and deallocate memory. Note the use of the constant **max_ints** in the **int_array** data type definition. **Max_ints** represents the maximum number of elements in an integer array. By defining an array data type with **max_ints** as the largest element, you can use an **int_array** pointer to point to an **integer** array of any size. You can adapt this method for any Pascal data type by substituting the desired data type in the constant declaration's **sizeof** function.

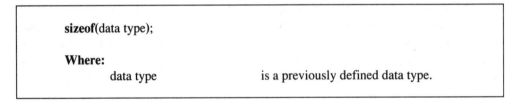

Figure 11-4. The Pascal sizeof function.

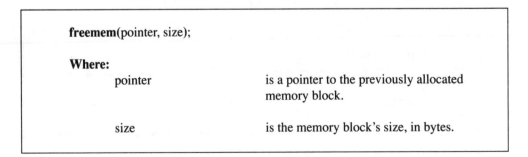

Figure 11-5. Deallocating memory with the freemem procedure.

Listing 11.2

```
{ list11-2.pas - Demonstrate allocating/deallocating blocks }
program alloc_dealloc;

const
      max_ints = 65520 div sizeof(integer);

type
      int_array = array[1..max_ints] of integer;

var
      i : integer;
      int_ptr : ^int_array;

begin
      getmem(int_ptr, 10 * sizeof(integer));
      for i := 1 to 10 do
            int_ptr^[i] := i;
      for i := 1 to 10 do
            writeln('int_ptr^[', i, '] = ', int_ptr^[i]);
      freemem(int_ptr, 10 * sizeof(integer));
end
```

***

You're now familiar with dynamic memory management and know how to allocate and deallocate both single data objects and blocks of memory. Chapter 12 tells you how to develop your own units to simplify your future programming tasks.

Chapter 12

Units

As you write more Pascal programs, you will find yourself repeating many of the same procedures and functions. Instead of recreating these routines each time you write a program, you can group many of them together to form a Pascal library called a **unit**.

Many of the sample programs in this book use procedures and functions that come with Turbo Pascal and QuickPascal. The majority of these routines are contained in Pascal's default unit called **system**. Other units included with Turbo Pascal and QuickPascal are **crt, dos, printer, graph** (Turbo Pascal only), **graph3** (Turbo Pascal only), **msgraph** (QuickPascal only), **overlay** (Turbo Pascal only), and **turbo3** (Turbo Pascal only). In addition to teaching you how to use these units, this chapter tells you how to work with the uses statement to create your own units. The chapter also discusses identifiers with the same name.

LESSON 79. The Uses Statement

In order to use a unit in a program, you must specify the unit's name in a **uses** statement. Figure 12-1 defines the structure of a **uses** statement. As this figure illustrates, you declare the name of the unit (or units) after the **uses** keyword. Once you specify a unit's name in a **uses** statement, all of the unit's procedures and functions are at your disposal.

---

uses unit identifier;

Where:

       unit identifier   is the Pascal unit's name. You can specify more than one unit by separating the units' names with commas.

Figure 12-1. The Pascal uses statement.

Listing 12.1 shows how the **crt** unit is used in an actual Pascal program. Although it only clears the screen and centers a message on the top display line, this program demonstrates how the Pascal **uses** statement functions.

Listing 12.1

```
{ list12-1.pas - Demonstrate the Pascal uses statement }
program uses_demo;

uses crt;

begin
     clrscr;
     gotoxy(28, 1);
     writeln('This Message Is Centered!');
end.
```

LESSON 80. Creating a Pascal Unit

Now that you know how a unit is used with a Pascal program, turn your attention to the details of writing a unit. Figure 12-2 defines the structure of a Pascal unit. Just as a program starts with a **program** statement, a unit starts with a **unit** statement. The purpose of the **unit** statement is to assign a name to the unit. Figure 12-2 also defines the construction of a **unit** statement.

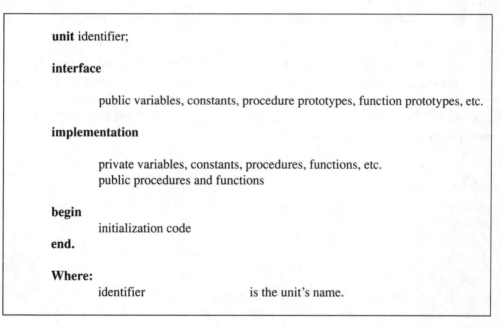

unit identifier;

interface

       public variables, constants, procedure prototypes, function prototypes, etc.

implementation

       private variables, constants, procedures, functions, etc.
       public procedures and functions

begin
       initialization code
end.

Where:
       identifier   is the unit's name.

Figure 12-2. The structure of a Pascal unit.

The second part of a Pascal unit is the **interface** section. You use the **interface** section to declare any variables, constants, data types, etc. that you want the main Pascal program to be able to use. The **interface** section also includes procedure and function prototypes for any of the unit's procedures and functions that can be called by the main Pascal program.

The third portion of a Pascal unit is the **implementation** section. You use the **implementation** section to declare any variables, constants, data types, etc. that won't be accessible to the main Pascal program. The **implementation** section also includes definitions for private procedures and functions as well as any procedures

173

and/or functions that you made public by specifying their prototypes in the **interface** section.

The final section of a Pascal unit is the initialization code. Like the program's main body, this code is contained in a **begin..end** block. The initialization code block uses a period (**.**) instead of a semicolon (**;**), however, to signify the end of the unit. Essentially, any program statements contained in the initialization code are executed before the main Pascal program. For example, a serial communications unit might have an initialization section that quite literally initializes the serial interface.

Listing 12.2 demonstrates how a Pascal unit is actually constructed. Note how the two public procedures' prototypes (**uppercase and lowercase**) are defined in the unit's **interface** section and how an empty **begin..end** block is specified for the unit's initialization code. If you examine the unit's code, you will quickly deduce that the unit's **uppercase** procedure converts strings to all uppercase and the unit's **lowercase** procedure converts strings to all lowercase.

Listing 12.2

```
{ list 12-2.pas - Demonstrate how a Pascal unit is written }
unit uplow;

interface

procedure uppercase(var s : string);
procedure lowercase(var s : string);

implementation

const
    offset = integer('a') - integer('A');

function testupper(c : char) : boolean;
begin
    if (c >= 'A') and (c <= 'Z') then
        testupper := true
    else
        testupper := false;
```
continued...

174

...from previous page
```
end;

function testlower(c : char) : boolean;
begin
      if (c >= 'a') and (c <= 'z') then
            testlower := true
      else
            testlower := false;
end;

procedure uppercase(var s : string);
var
      i : integer;

begin
      for i := 1 to length(s) do
            if testlower(s[i]) then
                  s[i] := char(integer(s[i]) - offset);
end;

procedure lowercase(var s : string);
var
      i : integer;

begin
      for i := 1 to length(s) do
            if testupper(s[i]) then
                  s[i] := char(integer(s[i]) + offset);
end;

begin
end.
```

Listing 12.3 demonstrates how the **uplow** unit is used in an actual program. As with any of Pascal's supplied units, you make **uplow** accessible to the main Pascal program by specifying its name in a **uses** statement. With the string conversion statements available in the **uplow** unit, the demonstration program simply converts a string of lowercase characters to uppercase and a string of uppercase characters to lowercase.

Listing 12.3

```
{ list12-3.pas - uplow demonstration program }
program uplow_demo;

uses uplow;

var
      s1, s2 : string;

begin
      s1 := 'this will be converted to all uppercase';
      s2 := 'THIS WILL BE CONVERTED TO ALL LOWERCASE';
      uppercase(s1);
      lowercase(s2);
      writeln(s1);
      writeln(s2);
end.
```

LESSON 81. Identifiers with the Same Name

Sooner or later you're bound to write a program that has an identifier with the same name as one used in a unit. Obviously, having two or more identifiers with the same name can lead to some unexpected results if the identifiers aren't handled properly. Fortunately, Pascal provides a simple solution to work around these conflicts.

Figure 12-3 defines the format for distinguishing between a unit's identifier and an identifier either in the main program or another unit. As the figure shows, you make this distinction by preceding the identifier with its corresponding unit name. Think of the unit as a big record and the identifier as one of the record's field names.

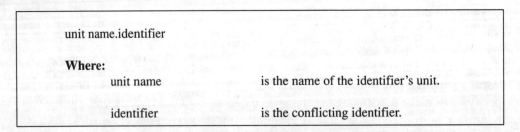

Figure 12-3. Conflicting identifier references.

Listing 12.4 demonstrates how conflicting identifiers are referenced in a Pascal program. This program makes use of the **uplow** unit, which was presented earlier in this chapter. To provide a conflicting identifier, the program in Listing 12.4 defines a new **uppercase** procedure that changes each character in a string to a (*). To use the **uppercase** procedure in **uplow**, the program references the procedure as **uplow.uppercase**.

Listing 12.4

```
{ list12-4.pas - Demonstrate how conflicting identifiers
  are referenced }

program conflict_ident;

uses uplow;

procedure uppercase(var s : string);
var
      i : integer;

begin
      for i := 1 to length(s) do
            s[i] := '*';
end;

var
      teststring : string;

begin
      teststring := 'I''m a test string!';
      writeln('teststring = ', teststring);
      uplow.uppercase(teststring);
      writeln('teststring = ', teststring);
      uppercase(teststring);
      writeln('teststring = ', teststring);
end.
```

***

You're now familiar with the **uses** statement and know how to create your own units to simplify your future programming tasks. Chapter 13 introduces you to strings.

Working with Strings

S tring data is probably the single most important data type to the Pascal programmer. This chapter introduces you to five important string-related functions and procedures: concatenation, copy, delete, insert, and pos. These routines will help you to manipulate string data.

LESSON 82. The String Concatenation Function

Like the Pascal string concatenation operator (+), which is described in Chapter 3, the Pascal string concatenation function, **concat**, combines one or more strings and returns the resulting string. Figure 13-1 defines the structure of the **concat** function. The concat function is simple to use. Suppose a program had an expression of **'string one'** + **'string two'**. The same expression could be rewritten as **concat('string one', 'string two')**.

```
concat(string expressions);

Where:
        string expressions          are one or more string expressions
                                     separated by a comma.
```

Figure 13-1. The Pascal concat function.

Listing 13.1 demonstrates how the Pascal **concat** function is used in an actual program. Note that the program concatenates two strings together with both the string concatenation operator and the string concatenation function. Both methods for concatenating strings return the same result.

Listing 13.1

```
{ list13-1.pas - Demonstrate the Pascal concat function }
program concat_demo;

var
     s1, s2, r1, r2 : string;

begin
     s1 := 'This is string 1 ';
     s2 := 'This is string 2 ';
     writeln('s1 + s2 = ', s1 + s2);
     writeln('concat(s1, s2) = ', concat(s1, s2));
end.
```

LESSON 83. The Pascal Copy Function

Because many string manipulations require extracting a portion of one string to form another string, Pascal provides the **copy** function. Figure 13-2 defines the structure of the **copy** function. The **copy** function returns a specified number of characters starting at a specified character position. If the specified character position exceeds the length of the string, then the **copy** function returns a null string. If the specified number of characters plus the specified character position exceeds the length of the string, then only the remaining string characters are returned.

180

copy(string, character position, number of characters);

Where:

string	is the source string.
character position	is the starting character position for the string to be copied.
number of characters	is the number of characters to be extracted.

Figure 13-2. The Pascal copy function.

Listing 13.2 demonstrates how the **copy** function is used in an actual Pascal program. The program extracts and displays a person's first name. The Pascal **copy** function can be a powerful tool for extracting a more pertinent piece of data from a large one.

Listing 13.2

```
{ list13-2.pas - Demonstrate the Pascal copy function }
program copy_demo;

var
     name, first : string;

begin
     name := 'John S. Doe';
    first := copy(name, 1, 4);
    writeln('First Name: ', first);
end.
```

LESSON 84. The Pascal Delete Procedure

Because a portion of a string often must be removed in order to form a shorter string, Pascal provides a procedure called **delete** for performing just such an operation. Figure 13-3 defines the structure of the **delete** procedure. The **delete** procedure removes a specified number of characters starting at a specified character position. If the character position is larger than the string's length, then nothing is removed from the string. If the number of characters plus the character position exceeds the length of the string, then only the actual number of remaining string characters is removed.

---

delete(string, character position, number of characters);

Where:

string	is the string from which to remove the substring.
character position	is the starting character position for the substring to be deleted.
number of characters	is the number of characters to be deleted.

Figure 13-3. The Pascal delete function.

Listing 13.3 demonstrates how the **delete** procedure is used in an actual Pascal program. The program removes the middle initial from a person's name.

Listing 13.3

```
{ list13-3.pas - Demonstrate the Pascal delete procedure }
program delete_demo;

var
      s : string;

begin
      s := 'John S. Doe';
      delete(s, 6, 3);
      writeln(s);
end.
```

LESSON 85.   The Pascal Insert Procedure

Although the **delete** procedure is certainly handy for removing unwanted characters from a string, what if the program requires characters to be inserted into a string?

Pascal offers the **insert** procedure to meet this need. Figure 13-4 defines the structure of the **insert** procedure. This procedure inserts a source string into a destination string starting at a specified character position. If the resulting string's length is greater than 255 characters, the string result is truncated on the right.

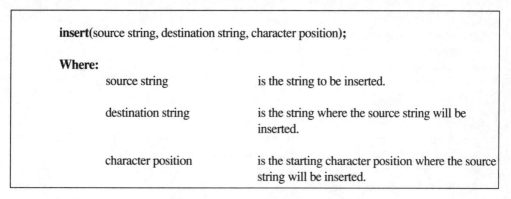

Figure 13-4. The Pascal insert procedure.

Listing 13.4 demonstrates how the Pascal **insert** procedure is used in an actual program. This program demonstrates the insertion task by simply inserting a middle initial into a name string.

Listing 13.4

```
{ list13-4.pas - Demonstrate the Pascal insert procedure }
program insert_demo;

var
     s : string;

begin
     s := 'John Doe';
     insert(' S.', s, 5);
     writeln(s);
end.
```

LESSON 86. The Pascal Pos Function

One of the most important string-handling routines for any program is a routine to perform string searches. Pascal provides the **pos** function to assist in implementing such a routine. Figure 13-5 defines the structure of the **pos** function. This function searches for one string in another. If the string is found in the string to be searched, then the **pos** function returns the search string's starting character position in the string to be searched. Otherwise, the **pos** function returns a value of 0.

---

pos(search string, string);

Where:

        search string   is the string for which to search.

        string   is the string to be searched.

Figure 13-5. The Pascal pos function.

Listing 13.5 demonstrates how the **pos** function is used in an actual Pascal program. To demonstrate how the Pascal **pos** function works, the program simply searches for a person's middle initial in a name string and displays the result.

Listing 13.5

```
{ list13-5.pas - Demonstrate the Pascal pos function }
program pos_demo;

var
     s : string;

begin
     s := 'John S. Doe';
     writeln('''S.'' is located at character position ',
pos('S.', s));
end.
```

***

You're now familiar with strings and know how to use string-related functions and procedures, such as concatenation, copy, delete, insert, and pos. Chapter 14 describes how data is input and output from the console.

Chapter **14**

Console Input/Output

The next three chapters are devoted to explaining how data is input and output with the Pascal programming language. This chapter explains how data is input and output from the console (keyboard and video display). It discusses the **write/writeln** and **read/readln** procedures, as well as formatted output.

LESSON 87.   The Write and Writeln Procedures

As their names imply, the Pascal **write** and **writeln** procedures are used to perform data output. The only real difference between the two procedures is that the **write** procedure does nothing after it has sent data to the output device, while the **writeln** procedure sends a new line (carriage return/line feed combination) to the output device. Figure 14-1 defines the **write** and **writeln** procedures.

```
write(argument list);
       or
writeln(argument list);

Where:
       argument list          is a list of one or more data items. A data item
                              can be a constant or a variable. Multiple data
                              items are separated by commas.
```

Figure 14-1. Using the write and writeln procedures for console output.

Each argument for a **write** or **writeln** procedure is a data item. This data item can be either a constant or a variable. You can specify multiple arguments by separating them with commas. When executed, the **write** or **writeln** procedure displays the data items' values in the order they appear in the argument list.

Listing 14.1 demonstrates how the **write** and **writeln** procedures are used in an actual program. The program displays a string and two integer values with the procedure first, followed by the same data items with the **writeln** procedure. The program clearly shows how the **writeln** procedure differs from the **write** procedure by generating a new line after displaying its arguments.

Listing 14.1

```
{ list14-1.pas - Demonstrate the write and writeln procedures }
program write_writeln_demo;

var
      i1, i2 : integer;

begin
      i1 := 11;
      i2 := 33;
      write('See the difference between write and writeln');
      write(i1, i2);
      writeln;
   continued...
```

...from previous page
```
    writeln('See the difference between write and
writeln');
    writeln(i1, i2);
end.
```

LESSON 88. The Read and Readln Procedures

As the **write** and **writeln** procedures provide the means to send data to the console, the **read** and **readln** procedures input data from the console. The **read** and **readln** procedures differ slightly in the way they function. The **read** procedure only reads the input until its data arguments have been filled. Any remaining data is used by the next **read** procedure. The **readln** procedure, on the other hand, keeps reading data until a new line is encountered. If any data remains after the **readln** procedure's data arguments have been filled, the remaining data is ignored. When entering data with the **read** and **readln** procedures, you must separate each data entry item by a space, tab, or carriage return.

Figure 14-2 defines how the **read** and **readln** procedures are used in a Pascal program. Like the **write** and **writeln** procedures, the **read** and **readln** procedures can have multiple data item arguments.

Unlike the **write** and **writeln** procedure arguments, however, the **read** and **readln** arguments must be variables. This requirement is obvious since a value can't be assigned to a constant.

---

read(argument list)**;**
    or
readln(argument list)**;**

Where:

argument list	is a list of one or more data items. Unlike **write** and **writeln** arguments, **read** and **readln** arguments must be variables. Multiple data items are separated by commas.

Figure 14-2. Using the read and readln procedures for console input.

Listing 14.2 demonstrates how the **read** and **readln** procedures are used in an actual Pascal program. This program demonstrates the differences between the **read** and readln procedures. The first **read** statement simply retrieves two integer values. The second set of **read** statements retrieves two integer values, but the operation is performed by two separate **read** statements. Note that if you enter both values as a response to the first **read** statement, the program won't request any further input. Instead, the second **read** statement uses the remaining data from the first **read** statement. Unlike the dual **read** statements, the program's **readln** statements require that the operator specifically enter the data one line at a time.

Listing 14.2

```
{ list14-2.pas - Demonstrate the read and readln procedures }
program read_readln_demo;

var
      i1, i2 : integer;

begin
      read(i1, i2);
      writeln('i1 = ', i1, ' i2 = ', i2);
      read(i1);
      writeln('i1 = ', i1);
      read(i2);
      writeln('i2 = ', i2);
      readln(i1);
      writeln('i1 = ', i1);
      readln(i2);
      writeln('i2 = ', i2);
end.
```

LESSON 89. Formatted Output

In addition to displaying unformatted data, the **write** and **writeln** procedures can also display data in a formatted mode. For example, you can tell either procedure to display a real number in a right-justified field with a specified width and number of decimal places. Figure 14-3 defines the format of a data item with either a **write** or **writeln** procedure. All formatted data items require a width specification. If the specified width is a positive number, the data item will be right-justified in a field of the specified width. If the specified width is a negative number, the data item will be left-justified in a field of the specified width. If the data item is wider than the specified width, it will be displayed as an unformatted data item. Figure 14-3 also shows that real number data items can optionally specify a number of decimal places.

```
data item:width
        or
real data item:width:decimal places
```

Where:

data item	is a data item of any previously defined type.
real data item	is any previously defined real number data type.
width	is the formatted field width.
decimal places	is an optional number of decimal places.

Figure 14-3. Formatted write and writeln data items.

Listing 14.3 demonstrates how formatted data items are specified in **write** and **writeln** statements. This program displays an account's name, number, and balance as a line of formatted data output. Note how the program uses a width specifier of **-20** to left justify the account's name and a width specifier of **10:2** to display the account balance with two decimal places.

Listing 14.3

```
{ list14-3.pas - Demonstrate formatted write and writeln output }
program formatted_write_writeln;

var
      number : integer;
      name : string;
      balance : real;
begin
      name := 'Cash';
      number := 101;
      balance := 100.31;
      writeln(name:-20, number:10, balance:10:2);
end.
```

***

You now know how to use the **write/writeln** and **read/readln** procedures and are familiar with formatted output. Chapter 15 examines preserving and retrieving data through text file input/output.

Chapter 15

Text File
Input/Output

This chapter tells you how to preserve and retrieve text files. It also introduces the concept of error trapping. Disk input/output is the preferred method for preserving and retrieving data to and from a permanent type of medium.

The Pascal programming language supports two basic types of disk files: text files and binary files. Data that is sent to and retrieved from text files is in the same format (ASCII strings) as data that is sent to and returned from the console. Consequently, you would have little trouble reading the data in a text file by simply listing it. However, data sent to and retrieved from a binary file uses the same format that Pascal uses to store data in the computer's internal memory. As a result, binary data files are virtually impossible to read.

LESSON 90. Text Files

The first step in opening a text disk file is to declare a variable of type **text** (a predefined data type just for working with text files). Figure 15-1 defines the format for declaring a **text** variable. As you can see from the figure, a **text** variable is declared like other variable types.

---

    var
        identifier **: text;**

    Where:
        identifier   is the **text** variable's name.

Figure 15-1. Declaring a text variable.

After you declare a **text** variable, the next step is to assign it a file name. The Pascal programming language provides a procedure called **assign** to accomplish this task. Figure 15.2 defines the structure of the **assign** procedure. To assign a file name to the text variable, specify the name of the text variable and the name of the file as the **assign** procedure's two arguments.

---

    assign(file variable, file name)**;**

    Where:
        file variable   is a previously declared file variable.

        file name   is the name of the data file.

Figure 15-2. The Pascal assign procedure.

Once you have assigned a file name to the file variable, you can open the disk file by using any one of three distinct Pascal procedures: **rewrite**, **reset**, or **append**. Although the **rewrite** procedure is capable of either creating a new file or opening an existing file, using it to open an existing file results in the loss of any data that already exists in the file. As a consequence, you should use the **reset** rather than the **rewrite** procedure to open an existing file. The contents of the data file are preserved when the file is opened by **reset**. The **append** procedure functions in the same way as the **reset** procedure except the **file pointer** (an internal pointer that points to the current location being accessed in a file) is set to the end of the file. By using the **append** procedure, you can open a file quickly to add data to the end of the file. Figures 15-3, 15-4, and 15-5 define the structure of the **rewrite**, **reset**, and **append** procedures.

Once you open a file, you can write to it or read from it using the Pascal **read**, **readln**, **write**, and **writeln** procedures. Figures 15-6, 15-7, 15-8, and 15-9 define these four procedures as they are used with text files. The only difference between using any one of these procedures with a disk file and with the console is that the disk file requires you to specify a file variable for the procedure's first argument. With the variable specified, Pascal is able to direct the data input/output to the proper file.

---

rewrite(file variable);

Where:
        file variable   is the variable for the file to be opened.

Figure 15-3. Opening a file with the rewrite procedure.

---

reset(file variable);

Where:
        file variable   is the variable for the file to be opened.

Figure 15-4. Opening a file with the reset procedure.

---

append(file variable);

Where:
        file variable   is the variable for the file to be opened.

Figure 15-5. Opening a file with the append procedure.

---

read(file variable, data variables);

Where:

file variable	is a variable from which the file can read the data.
data variables	are one or more data variables. Multiple data variables are separated by commas.

Figure 15-6. Reading file data with the read procedure.

---

readln(file variable, data variables);

Where:

file variable	is a variable from which the file can read the data.
data variables	are one or more data variables. Multiple data variables are separated by commas.

Figure 15-7. Reading file data with the readln procedure.

---

write(file variable, data items);

Where:

file variable	is a variable to which the file can write the data.
data items	are one or more constants or variables. Multiple data items are separated by commas.

Figure 15-8. Writing file data with the write procedure.

---

writeln(file variable, data items);

Where:

    file variable   is a variable to which the file can write the data.

    data items   are one or more constants or variables.
                                         Multiple data items are separated by commas.

Figure 15-9. Writing file data with the writeln procedure.

After a data file's input/output operations have been completed, you must close the file with the Pascal **close** procedure. Figure 15-10 defines the structure of the **close** procedure. You close a file by specifying its file variable as the **close** procedure's one and only argument.

---

close(file variable);

Where:

    file variable   is the variable for the file to be closed.

Figure 15-10. Closing a file with the close procedure.

Listing 15.1 demonstrates how a Pascal text file is accessed in an actual program. This program starts by opening a text file, writing 10 lines of data to the file, and closing the file. With the data safely stored away on disk, the program continues by re-opening the text file, reading and displaying the 10 lines of data, and then reclosing the file. Note the program's use of Pascal's **eof** function. It returns a value of **True** if a specified file's file pointer is located at the end of the file's data. Otherwise, the **eof** function returns a value of **False**. By using the **eof** function in a **while** loop, the program easily reads in all of the file's data. It continues to read data until **eof** returns a value of **True**.

Listing 15.1

```
{ list15-1.pas - Text file demonstration program }
program text_file_demo;
    continued...
```

...from previous page

```
var
      datafile : text;
      i : integer;
      s : string;

begin
      assign(datafile, 'textdemo.dat');
      rewrite(datafile);
      for i := 1 to 10 do
           writeln(datafile, 'This is data item no. ', i);
      close(datafile);
      reset(datafile);
      while not eof(datafile) do
      begin
           readln(datafile, s);
           writeln(s);
      end;
      close(datafile);
end.
```

LESSON 91.   Error Trapping

Although today's disk drives are reliable storage devices, errors do occur occasionally. Consequently, all but the simplest of data handling programs should provide at least a minimal amount of error handling. Pascal's normal input/output error handler generates a run-time error when an error occurs, but this crude error handling method is too simplistic for most programs.

Pascal provides the **{$I-}** and **{$I+}** compiler directives to assist you in dealing with input/output errors. A compiler directive tells the Pascal compiler to switch certain features on and off. With input/output directives, the **{$I-}** compiler directive tells Pascal not to generate run-time errors when an input/output error occurs. The **{$I+}** compiler directive tells Pascal to generate run-time errors whenever an input/output error occurs.

When the Pascal program is set to **{$I-}**, a call to the Pascal **ioresult** function can be used to determine if an input/output error has occurred. If **ioresult** returns a value of

0, the last input/output operation was returned without an error. If **ioresult** returns a non-zero value, the last input/output operation was returned with an error.

Listing 15-2 is a revised version of Listing 15-1. It utilizes the **{$I-}** and **{$I+}** compiler directives to provide a simple error handling routine. Although this program only displays a relevant error message, you could modify the program further to provide for a more sophisticated error handler.

Listing 15.2

```
{ list15-2.pas - Error handling demonstration program }
program error_handler_demo;

procedure errorhandler(s : string);
begin
      writeln(s);
      halt(1);
end;

var
      datafile : text;
      i : integer;
      s : string;

begin
      {$I-};
      assign(datafile, 'textdemo.dat');
      rewrite(datafile);
      {$I+};
      if ioresult <> 0 then
            errorhandler('Error opening file:
            textdemo.dat');
      for i := 1 to 10 do
      begin
            {$I-};
            writeln(datafile, 'This is data item no. ', i);
            {$I+};
```
continued...

...from previous page

```
            if ioresult <> 0 then
                errorhandler('Error writing file: textdemo.dat');
       end;
       {$I-};
       close(datafile);
       {$I+};
       if ioresult <> 0 then
            errorhandler('Error closing file:
            textdemo.dat');
    {$I-};
      reset(datafile);
    {$I+};
      if ioresult <> 0 then
            errorhandler('Error opening file:
            textdemo.dat');
      while not eof(datafile) do
      begin
            {$I-};
            readln(datafile, s);
            {$I+};
            if ioresult <> 0 then
                errorhandler('Error reading file:
                textdemo.dat');
            writeln(s);
      end;
      {$I-};
      close(datafile);
      {$I+};
      if ioresult <> 0 then
            errorhandler('Error closing file:
            textdemo.dat');
end.
```

***

You now know how to preserve and retrieve text data, and you understand the concept of error trapping. Chapter 16 examines binary file storage.

Chapter 16

Binary File
Input/Output

This chapter discusses typed and untyped binary data files—the most efficient way to store numeric data types. In a binary data file, data is stored on disk in the same format that it is stored in the computer's memory. Because a data item's internal binary representation almost always requires less memory than its ASCII string counterpart, storing data in a binary file greatly reduces the amount of disk space required to store the data.

Another benefit of storing data in binary files has to do with the fact that the Pascal program is fully aware of the size of a data item. For example, Pascal stores **integers** as two binary bytes. An ASCII string representation of an **integer** requires from one (as in **0**) to six (as in **-19999**) characters. Consequently, a Pascal program can never extract an **integer** accurately from a text file. Without first reading all of the preceding data items, the program doesn't know where the data item is located in a text file. The method of reading preceding data items in order to access data in a text file is called **sequential access**. Because the Pascal program knows just how large each data item is in a binary file, however, it can position the file pointer directly on a desired data item and either read its contents or replace it with a new data item. This method is called **random access**. It stands to reason that, in all but the simplest of files, the **random access** method is usually the preferred method for accessing data.

LESSON 92. Typed Binary Files

The Pascal programming language supports two types of binary files: typed binary files and untyped binary files. In this lesson, you will explore how typed binary files are used. Opening a typed binary file is almost identical to opening a text file. As with a text file, the first step in opening a binary file is to declare a file variable. Figure 16-1 defines the structure for declaring file variables for typed binary files. As this figure shows, a typed binary file variable declaration is similar to any other variable declaration.

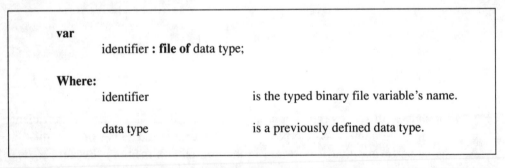

Figure 16-1. Declaring a typed binary file variable.

As with opening a text file, the next step in opening a typed binary file is to use the **assign** procedure to assign a file name to the file's variable. Once you've assigned a file name to a typed binary file variable, you can open the file with either the **rewrite** or the **reset** procedure. Data is read from a file with the **read** procedure and written to a file with the **write** procedure. Figure 16-2 defines the **read** procedure as it is used to read data from a typed binary file. Figure 16-3 defines the **write** procedure as it is used to write data to a typed binary file. As these figures show, all data items in a **read** or **write** argument list must be of the same data type as in the typed binary file's variable declaration. Like text files, typed binary files are closed with the **close** procedure.

If you used only the file-handling procedures described above, you could write a very efficient sequential access data file. In order to be able to randomly access a file, however, you need the assistance of the **seek** procedure and the **filepos** function.

You use the **seek** procedure to move a typed binary file's file pointer to a desired location. Figure 16-4 defines the structure of the **seek** procedure. As this figure shows, you use the second argument of the **seek** procedure to specify the record number for the file pointer's new location. Note that a file's first record is record 0 and not record 1. Record 1 is the second record in a typed binary file.

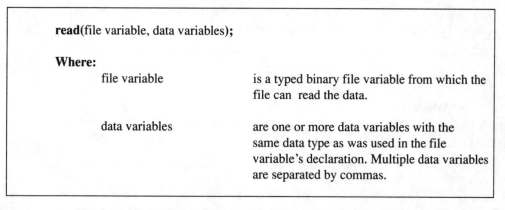

read(file variable, data variables);

Where:

file variable	is a typed binary file variable from which the file can read the data.
data variables	are one or more data variables with the same data type as was used in the file variable's declaration. Multiple data variables are separated by commas.

Figure 16-2. Reading typed binary file data with the read procedure.

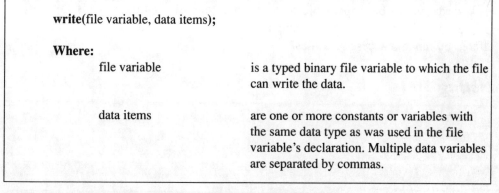

write(file variable, data items);

Where:

file variable	is a typed binary file variable to which the file can write the data.
data items	are one or more constants or variables with the same data type as was used in the file variable's declaration. Multiple data variables are separated by commas.

Figure 16-3. Writing typed binary file data with the write procedure.

seek(file variable, position);

Where:

file variable	is the typed binary file's variable.
position	is the record number to which to move the file pointer.

Figure 16-4. The Pascal seek procedure.

As its name implies, the Pascal **filepos** function returns the current record number for the file's current file pointer position. The value returned by the **filepos** function is of type **LongInt**. Figure 16-5 defines the structure of the **filepos** function. As this figure shows, the **filepos** function's sole argument is the typed binary file's variable.

filepos(file variable);

Where:

file variable	is the typed binary file's variable.

Figure 16-5. The Pascal filepos function.

Listing 16.1 demonstrates how a typed binary file can be used to perform random access. The program starts by creating a typed binary file of type **integer** and filling the file with dummy integer values. It continues by re-opening the file and reading and displaying the dummy values back in reverse order. Obviously, reading a file backwards would be impossible to do with a text file. Although this is a rather simple example of randomly accessing a data file, it clearly shows some of the power offered by random access data files.

Listing 16.1

```
{ list16-1.pas - Typed binary file demo }
program typed_bin_file;

var
      datafile : file of integer;
      i, rec : integer;
```
continued...

...from previous page

```
begin
      writeln('Writing demo file.....');
      assign(datafile, 'demofile.dat');
      rewrite(datafile);
      for i := 1 to 10 do
           write(datafile, i);
      close(datafile);
      write('Reading demo file backwards.....');
      reset(datafile);
      for i := 10 downto 1 do
      begin
           seek(datafile, i - 1);
           read(datafile, rec);
           write(rec, '...');
      end;
      close(datafile);
      writeln;
end.
```

LESSON 93. Untyped Binary Files

Although the typed binary files presented in the previous lesson are by far the most commonly used of the Pascal binary file types, you can also store data as an untyped binary file. Because an untyped binary file doesn't have a data type, data can be read from and written to the file without regard for its data type. Instead of reading and writing data in the form of constants and variables, an untyped file stores data in buffer areas.

The steps for opening an untyped binary file are similar to those for opening a typed binary file. The first step is to declare the file variable. Figure 16-6 defines the structure for declaring an untyped binary file. As this figure shows, the Pascal programming language provides a predefined data type called **file** that is used for declaring untyped binary file variables.

```
    var
            identifier : file;


    Where:
            identifier                        is the untyped binary file variable's name.


```

Figure 16-6. Declaring an untyped binary file variable.

Once you've declared the variable properly, you can open the untyped binary file by first using the **assign** procedure to assign a file name to the variable and then using the **rewrite** or **reset** procedure to open the file. You should be aware, however, that the **rewrite** and **reset** procedures interact differently with untyped binary files than with other Pascal file types. With untyped binary files, you can also use these two procedures to specify a record size.

Figures 16-7 and 16-8 define the structures of the **rewrite** and **reset** procedures as they are used with untyped binary data files. As these figures show, an untyped binary file will have a record length of 128 if the default record size argument is omitted.

```
    rewrite(file variable, record size);

    Where:
            file variable                     is the variable for the untyped binary file to
                                              be opened.

            record size                       is an optional record size for the untyped
                                              binary file. If the record size argument is
                                              omitted, a default record size of 128 will be
                                              used for the untyped binary file.


```

Figure 16-7. Opening an untyped binary file with the rewrite procedure.

---

reset(file variable, record size)**;**

Where:

file variable	is the variable for the untyped binary file to be opened.
record size	is an optional record size for the untyped binary file. If the record size argument is omitted, a default record size of 128 will be used for the untyped binary file.

Figure 16-8. Opening an untyped binary file with the reset procedure.

Because an untyped binary file doesn't have a data type associated with it, the Pascal **read** and **write** procedures can't be used to read from and write to an untyped binary file. Instead, Pascal offers the **blockread** and **blockwrite** procedures for dealing with these types of files. Figures 16-9 and 16-10 define the **blockread** and **blockwrite** procedures. As these figures show, the second argument is a pointer to a predeclared buffer area. This buffer area is simply an array that is big enough to hold the number of records defined in the procedure's third argument. The fourth argument for both procedures is optional and returns the actual number of records that the procedure reads or writes. After all of the read/write operations are completed, an untyped binary file is closed with the Pascal **close** procedure.

---

blockread(file variable, buffer, number of records, number read)**;**

Where:

file variable	is the variable for the untyped binary file to be read.
buffer	is a variable large enough to hold the block to be read. This variable is usually an array.
number of records	is the number of records to read.
number read	is the actual number of records read.

Figure 16-9. Reading data with the Pascal blockread procedure.

blockwrite(file variable, number of records, number written);

Where:

file variable	is the variable to which the untyped binary file is written.
buffer	is a variable large enough to hold the block to be written. This variable is usually an array.
number of records	is the number of records to write.
number written	is the actual number of records written.

Figure 16-10. Writing data with the Pascal blockwrite procedure.

Listing 16.2 demonstrates how untyped binary files are used in an actual program. Essentially, this program uses two untyped binary files to emulate the DOS COPY command. It sets up one untyped binary file with which to read the source file and another untyped binary file to which to write an exact copy. Although this program gets the job done, you should note that its lack of error trapping makes it unsuitable for daily use.

Listing 16.2

```
{ list16-2.pas - Untyped binary file demonstration}
program untyped_bin_file;

var
      sourcefile, destinationfile : file;
      buffer : array[1..4096] of char;
      length, no_written : word;
      file1, file2 : string;

begin
      write('Enter the name of the file to be copied: ');
      readln(file1);
      write('Enter the name to copy the file to: ');
```
continued...

...from previous page

```
      readln(file2);
      assign(sourcefile, file1);
      assign(destinationfile, file2);
      reset(sourcefile, 1);
      rewrite(destinationfile, 1);
      repeat
            blockread(sourcefile, buffer, 4096, length);
            blockwrite(destinationfile, buffer, length,
no_written);
      until (length = 0) or (length <> no_written);
      close(sourcefile);
      close(destinationfile);
end.
```

***

You are now familiar with typed and untyped binary data files. Chapter 17 discusses object-oriented programming in QuickPascal.

Chapter 17

Object-Oriented Programming in QuickPascal

W ithout a doubt, object-oriented programming is the hottest area in computer programming today. Unfortunately for both QuickPascal and Turbo Pascal programmers, this is where the two compilers part company. This chapter is devoted to presenting object-oriented programming as it applies to QuickPascal. The topics covered include: encapsulation, inheritance, and polymorphism. Chapter 18 discusses object-oriented programming as it applies to Turbo Pascal.

LESSON 94. Encapsulation

Traditional programming methods usually call for writing programs by first defining the program's code and then creating the data structures to go along with the resulting code. This leads to a second class status for program data. With object-oriented programming methods, however, code and data are considered equal partners. In an object-oriented program, the programmer defines object classes.

Object classes are similar to records, but they can also have their own procedures and functions. An object class's data fields are called **instance variables** and its procedures and functions are called **methods**. This merging of data fields, procedures, and functions into a single object class is called **encapsulation**. Encapsulation is one of the most important features that object-oriented programming offers.

Figure 17-1 defines the structure of an object class. An object class is defined like a record and it's field declarations are defined like record field declarations. The object class's method declarations are nothing more than procedure and function prototypes. Note that the order of the field and method declarations is unimportant; however, most programmers declare the object class's instance variables before defining its methods.

```
type
   class name = object
         field declaration;
         .
         .
         field declaration;
         method declaration;
         .
         .
         method declaration;
   end;

Where:
         class name                is the new object class's identifier.

         field declaration         is a valid field declaration.

         method declaration        is a procedure or function prototype.
```

Figure 17-1. Defining a QuickPascal object class.

Figure 17-2 defines an object class procedure, while Figure 17-3 defines an object class function.

The only difference between these procedures and functions and regular procedures or functions is the construction. All method definition names take the form of **object class.method name**. To return a value from an **object class** function, the return value is assigned to the method name, as shown in Figure 17-4.

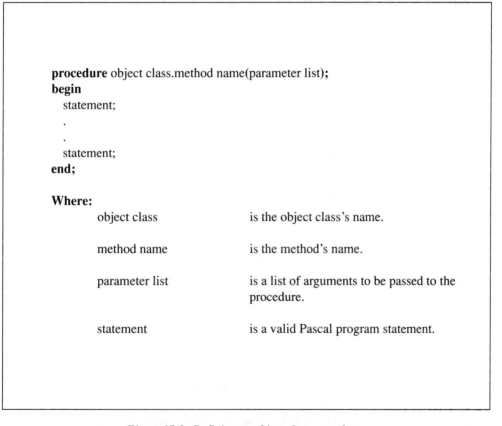

```
        procedure object class.method name(parameter list);
        begin
          statement;
          .
          .
          statement;
        end;

        Where:
                object class            is the object class's name.

                method name             is the method's name.

                parameter list          is a list of arguments to be passed to the
                                        procedure.

                statement               is a valid Pascal program statement.
```

Figure 17-2. Defining an object class procedure.

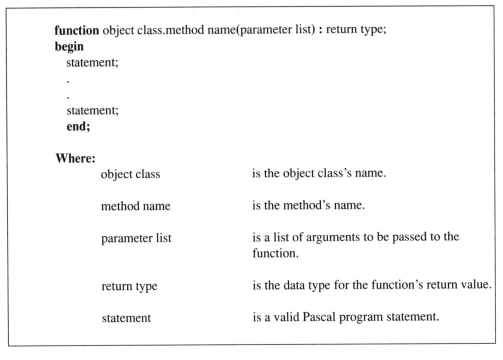

Figure 17-3. Defining an object class function.

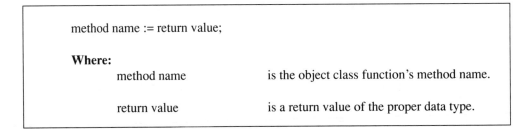

Figure 17-4. Returning values from an object class function.

As shown in Figure 17-5, an object or **class instance** is declared like other variables. With QuickPascal, all objects are dynamic data, and you must first allocate memory for them using the **new** procedure. Failure to allocate a spot in dynamic memory for an object will result in a run-time error. Because an object is a dynamically allocated piece of data, it must eventually be deallocated using the **dispose** procedure.

```
    var
       object name: object class;

  Where:
           object name                is a valid Pascal identifier.

           object class               is the desired object class's name.
```

Figure 17-5. Declaring a QuickPascal object.

Once you have declared and allocated an object, you can access its fields using the same methods as you use to access record fields. Figure 17-6 illustrates how an object's fields are referenced. Object-oriented programming techniques consider accessing an instance variable outside the object class's methods a violation because of data hiding. By not allowing you to directly access instance variables outside of the object class definitions, it insulates you from actually having to know the details about an object class. Instead, you should define object class procedures and functions for setting and retrieving instance variable values.

Figure 17-7 defines how an object class method is called. Other than preceding the **method name** with the **object name** and a period (**.**), there is no difference between a method call and a regular Pascal procedure or function call.

```
    object name.field name

  Where:
           object name                is the name of a previously declared class
                                       instance.

           field name                 is the name of one of the object class's fields.
```

Figure 17-6. Referencing instance variables.

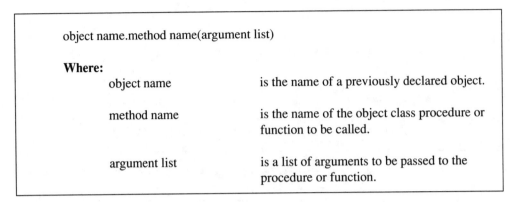

object name.method name(argument list)

Where:

object name	is the name of a previously declared object.
method name	is the name of the object class procedure or function to be called.
argument list	is a list of arguments to be passed to the procedure or function.

Figure 17-7. Calling an object's method.

There is one more requirement that you must understand in order to write a simple object-oriented program with QuickPascal. Whenever you reference one of an object class's instance variables or methods from within one of the same object class's methods, you must precede the **field name** or **method name** with the keyword **self** and a (.). That way the object class method knows to perform an operation on the same class instance.

Listing 17.1 demonstrates how you can use the object-oriented principle of encapsulation in a QuickPascal program. Note how methods have been defined for the program's object class to achieve data hiding. When using the object-oriented programming technique of data hiding, the instance variables are never directly accessed from outside of the object class. Data hiding is a useful technique for reducing errors and program development time in more complex object-oriented programs.

Listing 17.1

```
{ list17-1.pas - Encapsulation demo }
program encap_demo;

type
     employee = object
          name : string;
          age : integer;
          procedure init(n : string; a : integer);
          procedure display;
```
continued...

...from previous page

```pascal
            procedure setname(n : string);
            procedure setage(a : integer);
            function getname : string;
            function getage : integer;
      end;

procedure employee.init(n : string; a : integer);
begin
      self.name := n;
      self.age := a;
end;

procedure employee.display;
begin
      writeln('Employee''s name: ', self.name);
      writeln('Employee''s age: ', self.age);
end;

procedure employee.setname(n : string);
begin
      self.name := n;
end;

procedure employee.setage(a : integer);
begin
      self.age := a;
end;

function employee.getname : string;
begin
      getname := self.name;
end;

function employee.getage : integer;
begin
      getage := self.age;
end;
```

continued...

...from previous page

```
var
      e1, e2 : employee;

begin
      new(e1);
      new(e2);
      e1.init('John Smith', 33);
      e1.display;
      e2.setname('Jane Doe');
      e2.setage(28);
      writeln('Employee''s name: ', e2.getname);
      writeln('Employee''s age: ', e2.getage);
end.
```

LESSON 95. Inheritance

Although encapsulation is the cornerstone of object-oriented programming, inheritance makes it shine. Inheritance allows you to define an object class (called a subclass) based upon a previously defined object class (called a parent class).

Figure 17-8 illustrates how an object subclass is defined. Note that the only difference between defining a subclass and a parent class is the inclusion of the parent class's name following the **object** keyword in a subclass definition.

A subclass can use any instance variables and methods found in the parent class in addition to utilizing its own instance variables and methods. The instance variables and methods available to the subclass are a superset of the parent class's instance variables and methods.

Although a subclass can utilize all portions of the parent class, the reverse is not true. The parent class has no idea that the subclass even exists; therefore, it is impossible for the parent class to take advantage of any of the subclass's instance variables and methods.

```
    type
      class name = object(parent class)
            field declaration;
            .
            .
            field declaration;
            method declaration;
            .
            .
            method declaration;
      end;

    Where:
            class name              is the new object subclass's identifier.

            parent class            is the name of the subclass's parent class.

            field declaration       is a valid field declaration.

            method declaration      is a procedure or function prototype.
```

Figure 17-8. Defining a QuickPascal object subclass.

Listing 17.2 is a variation of Listing 17.1. This program uses inheritance to create a **secretary** subclass and an **executive** subclass for the **employee** parent class. Note how these new subclasses define their own unique instance variables and methods while retaining the instance variables and methods of the parent class. Also note how the **employee** parent class is never used to declare an object. Its only purpose is to serve as the parent class of the two new subclasses.

Listing 17.2

```
{ list17-2.pas - Inheritance demo }
program inherit_demo;

type
     employee = object
           name : string;
```
continued...

...from previous page

```
            age : integer;
            procedure init(n : string; a : integer);
      procedure display;
            procedure setname(n : string);
            procedure setage(a : integer);
            function getname : string;
            function getage : integer;
      end;

      secretary = object(employee)
            wpm : integer;
            procedure setwpm(w : integer);
            function getwpm : integer;
      end;

      executive = object(employee)
            keys : boolean;
            procedure setkeys(k : boolean);
            function getkeys : boolean;
      end;

procedure employee.init(n : string; a : integer);
begin
      self.name := n;
      self.age := a;
end;

procedure employee.display;
begin
      writeln('Employee''s name: ', self.name);
      writeln('Employee''s age: ', self.age);
end;

procedure employee.setname(n : string);
begin
```
    continued...

...from previous page

```
      self.name := n;
end;

procedure employee.setage(a : integer);
begin
      self.age := a;
end;

function employee.getname : string;
begin
      getname := self.name;
end;

function employee.getage : integer;
begin
      getage := self.age;
end;

procedure secretary.setwpm(w : integer);
begin
      self.wpm := w;
end;

function secretary.getwpm : integer;
begin
      getwpm := self.wpm;
end;

procedure executive.setkeys(k : boolean);
begin
      self.keys := k;
end;

function executive.getkeys : boolean;
begin
      getkeys := self.keys;
```
continued...

...from previous page

```
end;

var
      e1 : executive;
      e2 : secretary;

begin
      new(e1);
      new(e2);
      e1.init('John Smith', 33);
      e1.setkeys(true);
      e1.display;
      writeln('Executive Washroom Keys? ', e1.getkeys);
      e2.init('Jane Doe', 28);
      e2.setwpm(100);
      e2.display;
      writeln('Words per minute: ', e2.getwpm);
end.
```

LESSON 96. Polymorphism

Polymorphism is the ability to allow subclasses to redefine methods found in their parent classes. It is one of the most powerful tools at the object-oriented programmer's disposal. Polymorphic methods are called virtual methods. The keyword **override** follows the method's prototype in the subclass definition. Figure 17-9 shows the format for defining a subclass with virtual methods.

Object-oriented programming allows you to call not only the subclass's virtual methods, but also the parent class's inherited methods. Figure 17-10 defines the structure of calling a virtual method's inherited method. As this figure shows, an inherited method is called by simply preceding the method call with the keyword **inherited**.

Listing 17.3 demonstrates how polymorphism is used in an actual Pascal program. Listing 17.3 is more refined than Listings 17.1 and 17.2 as it defines the two subclasses' **display** methods as virtual methods. The program also demonstrates how inherited methods can still be called by calling the inherited parent class's **display** method from within the new virtual methods.

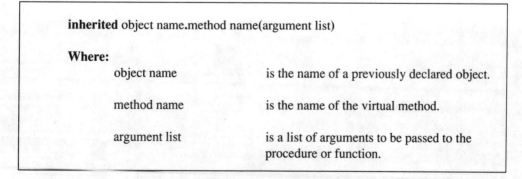

```
type
    class name = object(parent class)
            field declaration;
            .
            .
            field declaration;
            method declaration; override;
            .
            .
            method declaration; override;
            method declaration;
            .
            .
            method declaration;
    end;
```

Where:

class name	is the new object subclass's identifier.
parent class	is the name of the subclass's parent class.
field declaration	is a valid field declaration.
method declaration	is a **procedure** or **function** prototype.

Figure 17-9. Defining a QuickPascal polymorphic subclass.

```
inherited object name.method name(argument list)
```

Where:

object name	is the name of a previously declared object.
method name	is the name of the virtual method.
argument list	is a list of arguments to be passed to the procedure or function.

Figure 17-10. Calling an inherited method.

Listing 17.3

```
{ list17-3.pas - Polymorphism demo }
program poly_demo;

type
      employee = object
            name : string;
            age : integer;
            procedure init(n : string; a : integer);
            procedure display;
            procedure setname(n : string);
            procedure setage(a : integer);
            function getname : string;
            function getage : integer;
      end;

      secretary = object(employee)
            wpm : integer;
            procedure display; override;
            procedure setwpm(w : integer);
            function getwpm : integer;
      end;

      executive = object(employee)
            keys : boolean;
            procedure display; override;
            procedure setkeys(k : boolean);
            function getkeys : boolean;
      end;

procedure employee.init(n : string; a : integer);
begin
      self.name := n;
      self.age := a;
end;

procedure employee.display;
    continued...
```

...from previous page
```
begin
      writeln('Employee''s name: ', self.name);
      writeln('Employee''s age: ', self.age);
end;

procedure employee.setname(n : string);
begin
      self.name := n;
end;

procedure employee.setage(a : integer);
begin
      self.age := a;
end;

function employee.getname : string;
begin
      getname := self.name;
end;

function employee.getage : integer;
begin
      getage := self.age;
end;

procedure secretary.display;
begin
   inherited self.display;
      writeln('Words per minute:', self.wpm);
end;

procedure secretary.setwpm(w : integer);
begin
      self.wpm := w;
end;

function secretary.getwpm : integer;
begin
```
   continued...

...from previous page

```
        getwpm := self.wpm;
end;

procedure executive.display;
begin
        inherited self.display;
        writeln('Executive Washroom Keys? ', self.keys);
end;

procedure executive.setkeys(k : boolean);
begin
        self.keys := k;
end;

function executive.getkeys : boolean;
begin
        getkeys := self.keys;
end;

var
        e1 : executive;
        e2 : secretary;

begin
        new(e1);
        new(e2);
        e1.init('John Smith', 33);
        e1.setkeys(true);
        e1.display;
        e2.init('Jane Doe', 28);
        e2.setwpm(100);
        e2.display;
end.
```

***

You're now familiar with object-oriented programming in QuickPascal, and you understand the concepts of encapsulation, inheritance, and polymorphism. Chapter 18 examines object-oriented programming in Turbo Pascal.

Chapter 18

Object-Oriented Programming in Turbo Pascal

T his chapter explains how object-oriented programming is performed with Turbo Pascal. The topics covered include: encapsulation, inheritance, and polymorphism. There are a number of important differences between the way Turbo Pascal and QuickPascal implement object-oriented programming. Object-oriented programming with QuickPascal is covered in Chapter 17. If you have both QuickPascal and Turbo Pascal, you should go slowly and carefully through both chapters so as to not confuse the different approaches.

LESSON 97. Encapsulation

Traditional programming methods usually call for writing programs by first designing the program's code and then creating the data structures to go along with the resulting code. This leads to a second class status for the program data. With object-oriented programming, code and data are considered equal partners. In an object-oriented program, the programmer defines object classes. Object classes are similar to records, but they can also have their own procedures and functions. An object class's data fields are called **instance variables** and its procedures and functions are called **methods**. This merging of data fields, procedures, and functions into a single object class is called **encapsulation**. Encapsulation is one of the most important features that object-oriented programming offers.

Figure 18-1 defines the structure of an object class. An object class is defined like a record and its field declarations are defined like record field declarations. The object class's method declarations are nothing more than procedure and function prototypes. Note that the order of the field and method declarations is unimportant; however, most programmers declare the object class's instance variables before defining its methods.

Figure 18-2 defines an object class procedure, while Figure 18-3 defines an object class function. The only difference between these procedure and function definitions and a regular procedure or function definition is the construction. All method definition names take the form of **object class.method name**. To return a value from an object class function, the return value is assigned to the **method name**, as shown in Figure 18-4.

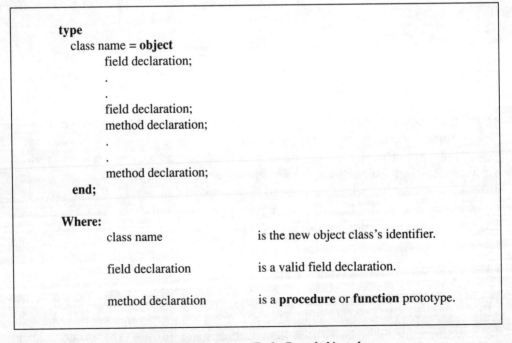

```
   type
     class name = object
           field declaration;

              .
              .
           field declaration;
           method declaration;

              .
              .
           method declaration;
     end;

Where:
           class name                    is the new object class's identifier.

           field declaration             is a valid field declaration.

           method declaration            is a procedure or function prototype.
```

Figure 18-1. Defining a Turbo Pascal object class.

```
    procedure object class.method name(parameter list);
    begin
      statement;
      .
      .
      statement;
    end;

Where:
        object class            is the object class's name.

        method name             is the method's name.

        parameter list          is a list of arguments to be passed to the
                                procedure.

        statement               is a valid program statement.
```

Figure 18-2. Defining an object class procedure.

```
    function object class.method name(parameter list) : return type;
    begin
      statement;
      .
      .
      statement;
    end;

Where:
        object class            is the object class's name.

        method name             is the method's name.

        parameter list          is a list of arguments to be passed to the
                                function.

        return type             is the data type for the function's return value.

        statement               is a valid program statement.
```

Figure 18-3. Defining an object class function.

```
        method name := return value;

Where:
        method name                 is the object class function's method name.

        return value                is a return value of the proper data type.
```

Figure 18-4. Returning values from an object class function.

Like an ordinary Pascal variable, an object (or **class instance**) must be declared before it can be used in a program. Figure 18-5 defines the declaration of an object. As the figure shows, an object declaration is identical to any other variable declaration.

Once you've defined an object, you can access its fields using the same format that you use to access record fields. Figure 18-6 defines the format for referencing an object's fields.

Object-oriented programming techniques consider accessing an instance variable outside of the object class's methods a violation because of data hiding. By not allowing you to directly access instance variables outside of the object class's definitions, it insulates you from actually having to know the details about an object class. Instead, you should define object class procedures and functions for setting and retrieving instance variable values.

```
    var
      object name : object class;

Where:
        object name                 is a valid Pascal identifier.

        object class                is the desired object class's name.
```

Figure 18-5. Declaring a Turbo Pascal object.

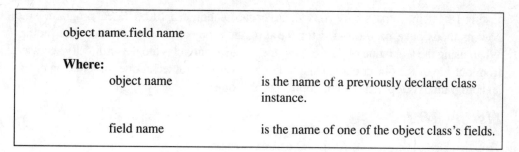

Figure 18-6. Referencing instance variables.

Figure 18-7 defines an object class method. Other than preceding the **method name** with the **object name** and a period (.) there is no difference between a method call and a regular Pascal procedure or function call.

Referencing an object class's instance variables or methods inside of the object class's methods is different from references outside of the object class: the object's name is not required (it would be impossible to specify an object's name from inside of a method). At times name conflicts can arise between the object's instance variable and method names and other identifiers used in the object class's methods. To prevent these name conflicts from occurring, you can precede the conflicting instance variable or method with the keyword **self** and a period (.). The **self** identifier is equivalent to using the object's name outside of the object class's methods.

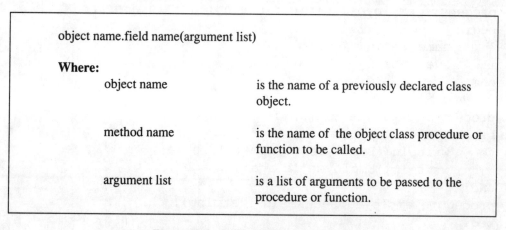

Figure 18-7. Calling an object's method.

Listing 18.1 demonstrates how you can use encapsulation in a Turbo Pascal program. Note how methods have been defined for the program's object class to achieve data hiding. When using the technique of data hiding, the instance variables are never directly accessed from outside of the object class. Data hiding is a very useful technique for reducing errors and program development time in more complex object-oriented programs.

Listing 18.1

```
{ list18-1.pas - Encapsulation demo }
program encap_demo;

type
      employee = object
            name : string;
            age : integer;
            procedure init(n : string; a : integer);
            procedure display;
            procedure setname(n : string);
            procedure setage(a : integer);
            function getname : string;
            function getage : integer;
      end;

procedure employee.init(n : string; a : integer);
begin
      name := n;
      age := a;
end;

procedure employee.display;
begin
      writeln('Employee''s name: ', name);
      writeln('Employee''s age: ', age);
end;
procedure employee.setname(n : string);
begin
      name := n;
end;
procedure employee.setage(a : integer);
```
continued...

...from previous page
```
begin
      age := a;
end;

function employee.getname : string;
begin
      getname := name;
end;

function employee.getage : integer;
begin
      getage := age;
end;

var
      e1, e2 : employee;

begin
      e1.init('John Smith', 33);
      e1.display;
      e2.setname('Jane Doe');
      e2.setage(28);
      writeln('Employee''s name: ', e2.getname);
      writeln('Employee''s age: ', e2.getage);
end.
```

LESSON 98. Inheritance

Although encapsulation is the cornerstone of object-oriented programming, inheritance makes it shine. Inheritance allows you to define an object class (called a subclass) based upon a previously defined object class (called a parent class). Figure 18-8 defines the structure of an object subclass. Note that the only difference between defining a subclass and a parent class is the inclusion of the parent class's name following the **object** keyword.

A subclass can use its own instance variables and methods, as well as any instance variables and methods in the parent class. The instance variables and methods available to the subclass are a superset of the parent class's instance variables and methods. Although a subclass can utilize all portions of the parent class, the reverse is not true—it is impossible for the parent class to take advantage of any of its subclass's instance variables or methods.

```
    type
      class name = object(parent class)
          field declaration;
          .
          .
          field declaration;
          method declaration;
          .
          .
          method declaration;
      end;
```

Where:

class name	is the new object subclass's identifier.
parent class	is the name of the subclass's parent class.
field declaration	is a valid field declaration.
method declaration	is a **procedure** or **function** prototype.

Figure 18-8. Defining a Turbo Pascal object subclass.

Listing 18.2 is a variation of Listing 18.1. It uses inheritance to create a **secretary** subclass and an **executive** subclass for the **employee** parent class. Note how these new subclasses define their own unique instance variables and methods while retaining the instance variables and methods of the parent class. Also note how the **employee** parent class is never used to declare an object. Its only purpose is to serve as the parent class of the two new subclasses.

Listing 18.2

```
{ list18-2.pas - Inheritance demo }
program inherit_demo;

type
    employee = object
          name : string;
          age : integer;
```
continued...

...from previous page

```
        procedure init(n : string; a : integer);
        procedure display;
        procedure setname(n : string);
        procedure setage(a : integer);
        function getname : string;
        function getage : integer;
    end;

    secretary = object(employee)
        wpm : integer;
        procedure setwpm(w : integer);
        function getwpm : integer;
    end;

    executive = object(employee)
        keys : boolean;
        procedure setkeys(k : boolean);
        function getkeys : boolean;
    end;
procedure employee.init(n : string; a : integer);
begin
    name := n;
    age := a;
end;

procedure employee.display;
begin
    writeln('Employee''s name: ', name);
    writeln('Employee''s age: ', age);
end;

procedure employee.setname(n : string);
begin
    name := n;
end;
```
continued...

...from previous page

```
procedure employee.setage(a : integer);
begin
      age := a;
end;

function employee.getname : string;
begin
      getname := name;
end;

function employee.getage : integer;
begin
      getage := age;
end;

procedure secretary.setwpm(w : integer);
begin
      wpm := w;
end;

function secretary.getwpm : integer;
begin
      getwpm := wpm;
end;

procedure executive.setkeys(k : boolean);
begin
      keys := k;
end;

function executive.getkeys : boolean;
begin
      getkeys := keys;
end;

var
      e1 : executive;
```
continued...

...from previous page

```
      e2 : secretary;

begin
      e1.init('John Smith', 33);
      e1.setkeys(true);
      e1.display;
      writeln('Executive Washroom Keys? ', e1.getkeys);
      e2.init('Jane Doe', 28);
      e2.setwpm(100);
      e2.display;
      writeln('Words per minute: ', e2.getwpm);
end.
```

LESSON 99. Polymorphism

Polymorphism is the ability to allow subclasses to redefine methods found in their parent classes. It is one of the most powerful tools at the object-oriented programmer's disposal.

Polymorphic methods are called virtual methods. The virtual keyword follows the method's prototype in both the parent class and the subclass. Once a method has been declared as **virtual**, it must remain **virtual** throughout all of the parent class's succeeding subclasses. Figure 18-9 defines a subclass with virtual methods.

Figure 18-9 also defines a special procedure called a **constructor**. A **constructor** is the same as a regular Pascal procedure except that the **procedure** keyword is replaced with the **constructor** keyword, and the **constructor** procedure performs a few internal tasks to enable the use of virtual methods in an object class. Note that any object class with virtual methods must have a **constructor**. Furthermore, each and every class instance must call the **constructor** before calling any of the class's other methods.

Failure to call the **constructor** first will most likely result in a fatal program error. Because the **constructor** must be called for each object, it is common practice to make the **constructor** an initialization routine for the object class.

```
type
  class name = object(parent class)
        field declaration;
        .
        .
        field declaration;
        constructor declaration;
        method declaration; virtual;
        .
        .
        method declaration; virtual;
        method declaration;
        .
        .
        method declaration;
    end;

Where:
        class name                is the new object subclass's identifier.

        parent class              is the parent class's identifier.

        field declaration         is a valid field declaration.

        constructor declaration   is the object class's constructor declaration.

        method declaration        is a procedure or function prototype.
```

Figure 18-9. Defining a Turbo Pascal polymorphic subclass.

Object-orented programming allows you to call not only the subclass's virtual methods, but also the parent class's inherited methods. Figure 18-10 defines the structure of a virtual method's inherited method. You call an inherited method by preceding the method name with the parent class's name and a period (.).

```
parent class.method name(argument list);
```

Where:

parent class	is the parent class's identifier.
method name	is the name of the virtual method.
argument list	is a list of arguments to be passed to the **procedure** or **function**.

Figure 18-10. Calling an inherited virtual method.

Listing 18.3 demonstrates how polymorphism is used in an actual Pascal program. It is more refined than Listings 18.1 and 18.2, as it defines the two subclasses' **display** methods as virtual methods. It also demonstrates how inherited methods can still be called by calling the inherited parent class's **display** method from within the new virtual methods. Also note how the subclasses' **constructors** serve two purposes: acting as Turbo Pascal's internal housekeeper and serving to initializing the object.

Listing 18.3

```pascal
{ list18-3.pas - Polymorphism demo }
program poly_demo;

type
     employee = object
          name : string;
          age : integer;
          constructor init(n : string; a : integer);
          procedure display; virtual;
          procedure setname(n : string);
          procedure setage(a : integer);
          function getname : string;
          function getage : integer;
     end;

     secretary = object(employee)
```
continued...

...from previous page

```
                wpm : integer;
                constructor init(n : string; a, w : integer);
                procedure display; virtual;
                procedure setwpm(w : integer);
                function getwpm : integer;
        end;

        executive = object(employee)
                keys : boolean;
                constructor init(n: string; a : integer; k : boolean);
                procedure display; virtual;
                procedure setkeys(k : boolean);
                function getkeys : boolean;
        end;

constructor employee.init(n : string; a : integer);
begin
        name := n;
        age := a;
end;

procedure employee.display;
begin
        writeln('Employee''s name: ', name);
        writeln('Employee''s age: ', age);
end;

procedure employee.setname(n : string);
begin
        name := n;
end;

procedure employee.setage(a : integer);
begin
        age := a;
end;
```
   continued...

...from previous page

```pascal
function employee.getname : string;
begin
      getname := name;
end;

function employee.getage : integer;
begin
      getage := age;
end;

constructor secretary.init(n : string; a, w : integer);
begin
      employee.init(n, a);
      wpm := w;
end;

procedure secretary.display;
begin
      employee.display;
      writeln('Words per minute:', wpm);
end;

procedure secretary.setwpm(w : integer);
begin
      wpm := w;
end;

function secretary.getwpm : integer;
begin
      getwpm := wpm;
end;

constructor executive.init(n : string; a : integer; k : boolean);
begin
      employee.init(n, a);
      keys := k;
```
continued...

...from previous page
```
end;

procedure executive.display;
begin
      employee.display;
      writeln('Executive Washroom Keys? ', keys);
end;

procedure executive.setkeys(k : boolean);
begin
   keys := k;
end;

function executive.getkeys : boolean;
begin
      getkeys := keys;
end;

var
      e1 : executive;
      e2 : secretary;
begin
      e1.init('John Smith', 33, true);
      e2.init('Jane Doe', 28, 100);
      e1.display;
      e2.display;
end.
```

LESSON 100. Dynamic Objects

You can dynamically allocate and deallocate objects with the **new** and **dispose** procedures. Figure 18-11 defines the structure for dynamically allocating objects with the **new** procedure. You can call an object's constructor as the **new** procedure's second argument, but a constructor is only required for object classes that utilize virtual methods. Although you can call the constructor as the **new** procedure's second argument, you can also call the constructor in another program statement after you have called the **new** procedure.

---

new(object pointer);
  or
new(object pointer, constructor call);

Where:

object pointer	is a pointer to the object to be dynamically allocated.
constructor call	is an optional constructor call. Because the object hasn't yet been assigned a name, only the constructor's method name is required for the constructor call.

Figure 18-11. Dynamically allocating an object with Turbo Pascal.

Figure 18-12 defines the structure for deallocating dynamically allocated objects with the **dispose** procedure. This figure also defines a call to a special **destructor** procedure specified as the **dispose** procedure's second argument. You declare a **destructor** procedure by substituting the **destructor** keyword for the **procedure** keyword in the object class definition. The destructor procedure is used to correctly deallocate dynamic memory and must be specified as the **dispose** procedure's second argument. To insure that Turbo Pascal deallocates the proper number of bytes, all dynamic objects should have a destructor. Furthermore, it is customary to specify any other cleanup chores within the destructor's definition.

---

dispose(object pointer);
  or
dispose(object pointer, destructor call);

Where:

object pointer	is a pointer to the object to be dynamically deallocated.
destructor call	is an optional destructor call. Note that only the destructor's method name is required for the destructor call.

Figure 18-12. Dynamically deallocating an object with Turbo Pascal.

Listing 18.4 demonstrates how objects are dynamically allocated in an actual Pascal program. This program is a revised version of Listing 18.3. Instead of using static objects, Listing 18.4 uses dynamically allocated objects to accomplish the same tasks. Note the use of destructors to ensure that the proper deallocation of dynamic memory is accomplished.

Listing 18.4

```
{ list18-4.pas. Dynamically allocated object demo }
program dynamic_demo;

type
      employee = object
            name : string;
            age : integer;
            constructor init(n : string; a : integer);
            destructor done; virtual;
            procedure display; virtual;
            procedure setname(n : string);
            procedure setage(a : integer);
            function getname : string;
            function getage : integer;
      end;

      secretary = object(employee)
            wpm : integer;
            constructor init(n : string; a, w : integer);
            destructor done; virtual;
            procedure display; virtual;
            procedure setwpm(w : integer);
            function getwpm : integer;
      end;

      executive = object(employee)
            keys : boolean;
            constructor init(n: string; a : integer; k : boolean);
            destructor done; virtual;
```
continued...

..from previous page

```
            procedure display; virtual;
            procedure setkeys(k : boolean);
        function getkeys : boolean;
        end;

constructor employee.init(n : string; a : integer);
begin
        name := n;
        age := a;
end;

destructor employee.done;
begin
end;

procedure employee.display;
begin
        writeln('Employee''s name: ', name);
        writeln('Employee''s age: ', age);
end;

procedure employee.setname(n : string);
begin
        name := n;
end;

procedure employee.setage(a : integer);
begin
        age := a;
end;

function employee.getname : string;
begin
        getname := name;
end;
```

continued...

...from previous page

```
function employee.getage : integer;
begin
      getage := age;
end;

constructor secretary.init(n : string; a, w : integer);
begin
      employee.init(n, a);
      wpm := w;
end;

destructor secretary.done;
begin
end;

procedure secretary.display;
begin
      employee.display;
      writeln('Words per minute:', wpm);
end;

procedure secretary.setwpm(w : integer);
begin
      wpm := w;
end;

function secretary.getwpm : integer;
begin
      getwpm := wpm;
end;

constructor executive.init(n : string; a : integer; k:
boolean);
 begin
      employee.init(n, a);
      keys := k;
end;
```

continued...

...from previous page

```
destructor executive.done;
begin
end;

procedure executive.display;
begin
      employee.display;
      writeln('Executive Washroom Keys? ', keys);
end;

procedure executive.setkeys(k : boolean);
begin
keys := k;

end;

function executive.getkeys : boolean;
begin
      getkeys := keys;
end;

var
      e1 : ^executive;
      e2 : ^secretary;

begin
      new(e1, init('John Smith', 33, true));
      new(e2, init('Jane Doe', 28, 100));
      e1^.display;
      e2^.display;
      dispose(e1, done);
      dispose(e2, done);
end.
```

***

You're now familiar with object-oriented programming as it applies to Turbo Pascal, and you understand the concepts of encapsulation, inheritance, and polymorphism.

Index

:= (assignment), 29-31
/ (real number), 36-37
- (set difference), 117-118
- (subtraction), 34-35
- (unary minus), 32-33
+ (addition), 33-34
+ (set union), 116-117
+ (string concatenation), 55-56
+ (unary plus), 31-32
* (multiplication), 35-36
* (set intersection), 118-119
< (less than), 60-61
<= (less than or equal to), 61-62
<= (set less than or equal to), 113-114
<> (not equal to), 57-58
<> (set not equal to), 112-113
= (equal to), 56-57
= (set equal to), 111-112
> (greater than), 58-59
>= (greater than or equal to), 59-60
>= (set greater than or equal to), 114-115
@ (address of), 152, 158

A

addr, 152
and (bitwise and), 48-49
and (logical and), 41-42
ANSI Pascal, xix
append, 192-193

arrays, 121-132, 140-144, 154-155
assign, 192, 200, 204

B

begin..end, 6
blockread, 205
blockwrite, 205-206
boolean, 19
booleans, 19-21
byte, 13

C

case, 75-76
char, 21
characters, 21-24
close, 195, 200
comment, 6-7
comp, 16
concat, 179-180
const, 8
constants, 3-4
copy, 180-181

D

data hiding, 213-216, 228-231
dec, 103-104
delete, 181-182
destructor, 241
dispose, 166-167, 212, 240-241
div (integer division), 38
double, 16

E

encapsulation, 209-216, 225-231

enumerated data types, 101-103
eof, 195
error handling, 196-198
extended, 16

F

file data type, 203-204
filepos, 201-202
for, 69-72
forward declarations, 85-88
freemem, 167-169
function return values, 83-85
functions, 7, 80-83, 157-163

G

getmem, 167-169
global variables, 91
goto, 77

H

hexadecimal numbers, 12

I

identifiers, 3
if, 72-74
implementation, 173-174
in (set in), 115-116
inc, 104-105
inheritance, 216-220, 231-235
inherited, 220-221
insert, 182-183
instance variables, 210, 226
integer, 13

integers, 11-15
interface, 173-174
ioresult, 196-197

K

keywords, 2

L

local variables, 88-91
longint, 13

M

methods, 210-226
mod (remainder), 39-40
multi-dimensional arrays, 126-130

N

named constants, 5
new, 166-167, 212, 240-241
nil, 152-153
not (bitwise negation), 46-47
not (logical negation), 40-41

O

operators, 4-5
or (bitwise or), 49-50
or (logical or), 43-44
ordinal data types, 103
override, 220-221

P

parameters, 80, 93-95, 131-132
parentheses, 63-64

pointers, 151-163
polymorphism, 220-224, 235-240
pos, 183-184
precedence, 62-64
pred, 106-107
procedures, 7, 80-83, 157-163
program, 8

R

random access, 200, 202
read, 187-188, 193-194, 200-201
readln, 187-188, 193-194
real, 16
real numbers, 16-19
records, 133-144, 154-156
recursion, 97-99
repeat, 67-69
reserved words, 2
reset, 192-193, 200, 204
rewrite, 192-193, 200, 204

S

scope, 91-93, 96
seek, 201-202
self, 214, 229
sequential access, 200
sets, 110-111
shl (bitwise shift left), 52-53
shortint, 13
shr (bitwise shift right), 53-54
single, 16
sizeof, 167-168
statements, 6

string, 24
strings, 24-27
subranges, 108-110
succ, 107-108

T

text data type, 192
typed constants, 14, 17-18, 20, 23, 26, 89-91, 125-126, 128, 139-140

U

unit, 173
units, 171-178
uses, 172

V

var, 8
variables, 4, 13, 19-20, 22-23, 25, 88-91, 157-160
variant records, 145-150
virtual, 235-236

W

while, 65-67
white space, 9
Wirth, Niklaus, xix
with, 137-139
word, 13
write, 185-190, 193-194, 200-201
writeln, 185-190, 193-195

X

xor (bitwise exclusive or), 51-52
xor (exclusive or), 44-45